W9-ABG-158

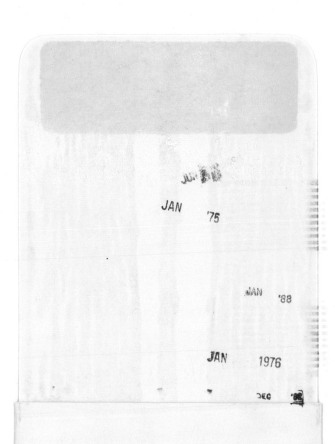

MEXICO
IN AMERICAN AND
BRITISH LETTERS

A Bibliography of Fiction and Travel Books,
Citing Original Editions

Compiled by
DREWEY WAYNE GUNN

The Scarecrow Press, Inc.
Metuchen, N.J.   1974

Library of Congress Cataloging in Publication Data

Gunn, Drewey Wayne, 1939-
    Mexico in American and British letters.

    1. American literature--Bibliography. 2. English
literature--Bibliography. 3. Mexico in literature--
Bibliography. 4. Mexico--Description and travel--
Bibliography. I. Title.
Z1225.G85   016.820'8'032   73-20354
ISBN 0-8108-0692-4

Copyright 1974 by Drewey Wayne Gunn

TABLE OF CONTENTS

FOREWORD

The user of this bibliography may be surprised at
how much Mexico has figured in the literature of the United
States and Great Britain, especially when he notes the names
of several of our most prominent writers. Others may be
surprised at how little the country, next door to the States
and one of the richest cultures of the world, seems to have
mattered, especially in comparison with the Continent's
great influence, to the development of American and British
letters. Either way, Mexico has still had a steady, small
but significant influence upon our literature since the country
was opened to visitors as a result of the War for Independence, 1810-1821. Even during the three hundred years in
which Spain had sealed off her empire, writers often darted
in for a look; indeed, the first general survey of the country
was written by an Englishman (see entry 747).

What interested these authors? There were countless matters, ranging from the mundane to (more usually)
the exotic. The Indian culture attracted many: the great
civilizations of the past, especially the moment when the
Aztecs confronted Cortés, have become the basis for some
fifty-three romances, and the ruins of their civilizations have
brought in scores; the primitive life--relatively speaking--
of their modern descendants often seemed a solution to
visitors overwhelmed by modern life (note 661 for example).
Mineral wealth--first gold and silver and later oil--stirred
the imagination, and occasionally even agriculture interested
some. Then there were the many stirring moments in
modern Mexican history: the War for Independence; the
Texas rebellion, 1836-1837, and the Mexican-American War,
1846-1848, in which Mexico was halved; the conflict between
Benito Juárez and Maximilian, 1862-1867, responsible for
at least eight personal narratives and some thirteen novels;
the Revolution of 1910, reflected in countless works; and the
excitement of the cultural renaissance of the 1920's, particularly that generated by the muralists. Americans especially were intrigued by the Mexican past of Texas

and the new Southwest (the British for some reason were likewise fascinated with stories of Texas): we have some twenty-two accounts of visits to California before 1846 and at least seventeen novels and dramas reflecting the period; seventeen accounts of life on the Santa Fe trail and elsewhere in New Mexico and twelve novels and dramas; twelve accounts of visits to Texas before 1836 and fourteen novels about the settlement and war of secession. Out of the Mexican-American War itself fifty-five journals and twenty-two novels have so far been published.

Responses to Mexico were varied. Quite often it was viewed as a dangerous place, a setting for murder and intrigue. Many went into a kind of trauma from the alien world which they found, hating and fearing the place. But almost as many described it as a kind of paradise. And some writers even managed to stay fairly balanced in their appraisals. Often, the visitor viewed the country as a place of escape from his own culture or as at least "another country" from which to review his past. All travel books were of course written from actual observations. Fiction, poetry, and drama often came from personal experiences, but some works, especially historical romances, were products of an author's reading alone. Romancers writing about Texas and the new Southwest generally resided in the area, but probably only those in New Mexico could find the old culture still somewhat intact.

Relatively little attention has been paid to the interrelations of the cultures. These two checklists of fiction and personal observations grew as a necessary sideline to my own study, American and British Writers in Mexico, 1556 to 1969, to be published by the University of Texas Press. (A third list, of histories and biographies, was abandoned since bibliographies are available here. One grieves to omit, however, the names of William H. Prescott, Lesley Simpson, and even Hammond Innes.) The few prior studies and bibliographies (listed below), the invaluable Book Review Digest, Cumulative Book Index, the Library of Congress and the British Museum printed catalogues (against which I checked all titles), miscellaneous standard bibliographies, and many lucky accidents went into their compilation. Titles were gathered primarily through the resources available at the University of North Carolina library in Chapel Hill, the Texas A&I University library in Kingsville, and the Royal Library of Copenhagen. The first edition is listed except in a few cases where no information was available (and a special situation for 457); subsequent editions are

given only when the material was significantly altered.
Spelling is that of the original; punctuation is my own.
Annotations were made in Copenhagen and are thus more
limited than I desired.

I appreciate greatly the help of a number of my col-
leagues and friends: Norma Beth Drake, English instructor
at Texas Southmost College; Kent T. Fields, business professor at A&I; Helen Haydon, professor of English at A&I;
Fredericka Martin of Cuernavaca; Daniel W. Patterson,
professor of English at North Carolina; Orlan Sawey, professor of English at A&I; and Patricia Smith, research
assistant. R. R. Hinojosa-Smith, professor of Spanish at
A&I, gave me the encouragement to put the lists together in
usable form. I hope readers will help me add new titles,
expand annotations, and correct any errors which may have
crept in: I can always be reached in care of the postmaster,
Wentworth, North Carolina 27375.

Drewey Wayne Gunn

Copenhagen: 8 June 1973

PRIOR BIBLIOGRAPHIES AND STUDIES

Babcock, Charles Edwin, Catherine M. Rooney, and Leila Fern. Children's Books in English on Latin America. Washington: Pan American Union, 1941.

Barrett, Ellen C. Baja California: A Bibliography of Historical, Geographical, and Scientific Literature Relating to the Peninsula of Baja California and to Adjacent Islands in the Gulf of California and the Pacific Coast. 2 v. Los Angeles: Bennett & Marshall, 1957-1967.

Bassols Batalla, Angel. Bibliografía geográfica de México. México: 1955.

Cox, Edward Godfrey. A Reference Guide to the Literature of Travel, Including Voyages, Geographical Descriptions, Adventures, Shipwrecks, and Expeditions. 2 v. Seattle: University of Washington, 1935-1938.

Estes, Mary Caroline. "American Travellers in Mexico, 1810-1940." Unpublished thesis, University of Texas, 1961.

Gardiner, Clinton Harvey. "Foreign Travelers' Accounts of Mexico, 1810-1910." Americas, VIII (January 1952), 321-351.

Mayer, William. Early Travellers in Mexico, 1534 to 1816. México: Cvltvra, 1961.

Robinson, Cecil. With the Ears of Strangers: The Mexican in American Literature. Tucson: University of Arizona, 1963.

Sturgis, Cony. The Spanish World in English Fiction: A Bibliography. Boston: F. W. Faxon, 1927.

1

Wilgus, Alva Curtis. Latin America in Fiction: A Bibliography of Books in English for Adults. Washington: Pan American Union, 1941.

Williams, Stanley T. The Spanish Background of American Literature. 2 v. New Haven: Yale University, 1955.

Woodcock, George. "Mexico and the English Novelist." Western Review, XXI (August 1956), 21-32.

Zelman, Donald Lewis. "American Intellectual Attitudes toward Mexico, 1908-1940." Unpublished dissertation, Ohio State University, 1969.

A CHECKLIST OF AMERICAN AND BRITISH
FICTION, POETRY, AND DRAMA ABOUT MEXICO,
AS WELL AS SOME RETOLD LEGENDS AND
FICTIONALIZED BIOGRAPHIES (1805-1972)

1 Aiken, Conrad Potter. A Heart for the Gods of Mexico.
   London: M. Secker, 1939. Collected Novels. New
   York: Holt, Rinehart & Winston, 1964.
     Short novel about the journey of three Americans
     to Cuernavaca in order for one to obtain a divorce.
     It is based rather closely upon the American poet's
     own visit in 1937; see 551.

2 Allen, Dexter. Coil of the Serpent. New York:
   Coward-McCann, 1956.

3 _____ . Jaguar and the Golden Stag. New York:
   Coward-McCann, 1954.

4 _____ . Valley of Eagles. New York: Coward-
   McCann, 1957.
     Trilogy [2-4] about Netzahualcoyotl, an Aztec
     ruler, from his rise to power until a few years
     after Cortés's arrival.

5 Anderson, Maxwell. Night over Taos: A Play in Three
   Acts. New York: S. French, 1932.
     Verse drama about New Mexico during the Mexi-
     can-American War.

6 Anderson, Sherwood. Sherwood Anderson's Memoirs.
   New York: Harcourt, Brace, 1942.
     "Mexican Night" (short story): comedy about the
     way some American journalists frighten their fel-
     low tourists. The story is quite different from
     the essay printed in the critical edition (see 556).

7 Anthony, Wilder. Star of the Hills. London: W. Collins, 1926.

3

Romance of California during the Mexican-American War.

8 Armer, Laura Adams. The Forest Pool. New York, Toronto: Longmans, Green, 1938.
Children's story about the adventures of two Mexican boys.

9 Arnold, Elliott. The Time of the Gringo. New York: Knopf, 1953.
Novel centering around the rise to power of Manuel Armijo, governor of New Mexico, just before the Mexican-American War.

10 Atherton, Gertrude Franklin. (a) Before the Gringo Came. New York: J. S. Tait, 1894. (b) The Splendid Idle Forties: Stories of Old California. New York, London: Macmillan, 1902.
Short stories.

11 Austin, Mary Hunter. Isidro. Boston: Houghton Mifflin, 1905.
Historical romance of the life of a Mexican boy in California, dedicated to the Church by his father but in love with a young girl. See also 564.

12 Baerlein, Henry Philip Bernard. The House of the Fighting-Cocks. London: L. Parsons, 1922; New York: Harcourt, Brace, 1923.
Novel about the rather eccentric education of a Mexican youth during the time of Maximilian.
The English author spent some years in Mexico; see 566.

13 Baggett, Samuel G. Gods on Horseback. New York: McBride, 1952.
Romance of the Spanish Conquest seen from the Aztecs' side.

14 Bagley, Desmond. The Vivero Letter. London: Collins, 1968.
Mystery involving an Englishman's expedition to ruins in Yucatán.

15 Baker, Bertha Belle. Our Lady of Guadalupe, and Other Stories. Los Angeles: Graphic, 1941.

16   Baker, Betty. The Blood of the Brave. New York:
     Harper & Row, 1966.
         Novel for teenagers about a Spanish boy who was
     a member of Cortés's troops.

17   Baker, Charlotte. Hope Hacienda. New York: Crowell,
     1942; London: Hutchinson, 1949.
         Novel for teenagers about the adjustments of the
     young members of a family, of mixed Mexican and
     American backgrounds, to life together after the
     death of both parents.

18   _____. House of the Roses. New York: Dutton,
     1942.
         Mystery set in Mexico City during World War II.

19   _____. A Sombrero for Miss Brown. New York:
     Dutton, 1941.
         Mystery about the romantic adventures of an
     American schoolteacher in search of her lost
     brother.

20   Baker, Dorothy Dodds. Our Gifted Son. Boston:
     Houghton Mifflin, 1948; London: V. Gollancz, 1949.
         Novel about the problems of a sensitive Mexican
     youth, student at Harvard, who returns home
     after his mother's mysterious death.

21   Baker, Karle Wilson (pseud. Charlotte Wilson). Star
     of the Wilderness. New York: Coward-McCann,
     1942.
         Novel of the Texas secession.

22   Bannon, Laura. Manuela's Birthday in Old Mexico.
     Chicago: Whitman, 1939.
         Children's story about a girl's fifth birthday.

23   _____. Watchdog. Chicago: Whitman, 1948.
         Children's story about a Mexican boy.

24   Barnum, Frances Courtenay Baylor. Juan and Juanita.
     Boston: Ticknor, 1888.
         Children's story.

25   Baron, Alexander. The Golden Princess. London:
     Cape, 1954; New York: Washburn, 1954.

Romance about La Malinche, Cortés's Indian mistress.

26 Barrett, Monte. Sun in Their Eyes: A Novel of Texas
in 1812. Indianapolis: Bobbs-Merrill, 1944; London:
S. Paul, 1948.
Novel of violence.

27 Barry, Jane. Maximilian's Gold. Garden City:
Doubleday, 1966; London: V. Gollancz, 1967.

28 Bartlett, Paul. When the Owl Cries. New York:
Macmillan, 1960.
Novel about the effects of the Mexican Revolution
upon a family of the hacienda class. The American author lived many years in Mexico.

29 Bartlett, Virginia Stivers. Mistress of Monterey.
Indianapolis: Bobbs-Merrill, 1933.
Novel about California at the end of the 18th century, centering around Pedro Fages, the governor,
and Father Junípero Serra.

30 Bassing, Eileen Johnston. Where's Annie? New York:
Random House, 1963; London: Mayflower, 1965.
Novel about the life of expatriates, particularly
an American writer and an American artist.

31 Bates, Ralph. The Fields of Paradise. New York:
Dutton, 1940; London: J. Cape, 1941.
Novel about the overthrow of a petty Mexican
tyrant.

32 Baum, Vicki. Headless Angel. Garden City: Double-
day, 1948; London: M. Joseph, 1948.
Romance about a German countess who lived in
Mexico with her Spanish lover for several years
before the War for Independence. The author was
German-born.

Baylor, Frances Courtenay. See Barnum, F.C.B.

33 Beals, Carleton. Black River. Philadelphia, London:
Lippincott, 1934; London: V. Gollancz, 1935.
Fictional examination of the exploitation of Mexican
oil fields by American investors. The author was
an American journalist who lived many years in
Mexico; see 582-586.

34   . The Stones Awake: A Novel of Mexico.
   Philadelphia, London: Lippincott, 1936.
   Novel about a Mexican woman's participation in the
   Mexican Revolution.

35   . Stories Told by the Aztecs before the Span-
   iards Came. New York, London: Abelard-Schuman,
   1970.
   Legends retold for young people.

36 Behn, Harry. The Two Uncles of Pablo. New York:
   Harcourt, Brace, 1959; London: Macmillan, 1960.
   Children's story about the experiences of a Mexican
   mountain boy who comes to live in a village.

37 Beim, Lorraine, and Jerold Beim. The Burro That Had
   a Name. New York: Harcourt, Brace, 1939.
   Children's story about a Mexican boy.

38 Bellamy, Frank Rufus (pseud. Francis R. Bellamy).
   Spanish Faith: A Romance of Old Mexico and the Car-
   ibbean. New York: Harper, 1926.
   Historical romance about an American's love of a
   Spanish woman and his subsequent adventures.

39 Bellow, Saul. The Adventures of Augie March. New
   York: Random House, 1953; London: Weidenfeld &
   Nicolson, 1954.
   Picaresque novel, the middle part of which concerns
   expatriate life in Cuernavaca and an imaginary town
   modelled on Taxco, with a glimpse of Leon Trotsky.
   The American author visited Mexico in 1940.

40   . Mosby's Memoirs, and Other Stories. New
   York: Viking, 1968; London: Weidenfeld & Nicolson,
   1969.
   "Mosby's Memoirs" (short story): thoughts of a
   man, in Oaxaca and at Mitla, concerning the Euro-
   pean portion of his autobiography.

41 Beresford, Marcus (pseud. Marc Brandel). The Bar-
   riers Between. New York: Dial, 1949; London: Eyre
   & Spottiswoode, 1950.
   Psychological novel about the effect on an American
   commercial artist of his attack on another man.

42 Berle, Milton, and John Roeburt. Earthquake. New
   York: Random House, 1959.

          Novel about the life of expatriates in a small town, which is ruined by an earthquake.

43   Bird, Robert Montgomery. Calavar, or The Knight of the Conquest: A Romance of Mexico. Philadelphia: Carey, Lea & Blanchard, 1834. Abdalla the Moor and the Spanish Knight: A Romance of Mexico. London: A. K. Newman, 1835.

44   _____. The Infidel, or The Fall of Mexico. Philadelphia: Carey, Lea & Blanchard, 1835. Cortes, or The Fall of Mexico. London: R. Bentley, 1835.
        Two romances [43-44] of the Conquest. The American author planned a trip to Mexico but never made it.

45   Birne, Henry. Wait for the New Grass. New York: St. Martin's, 1961.
        Novel about an American veterinarian's work against hoof-and-mouth disease and his involvement with the Mexican people. It is based on the author's similar experiences.

46   Birney, Hoffman. Eagle in the Sun. New York: Putnam's, 1935.
        Novel about two Americans in the Mexican-American War.

47   Bishop, William Henry. Tons of Treasure: A Tale of Adventure and Honor; Being a New and Improved Edition of "The Yellow Snake." New York: Street & Smith, 1902.
        The author visited Mexico; see 606.

48   Blacker, Irwin Robert. Taos. Cleveland: World, 1959; London: Cassell, 1960.
        Novel about the rebellion of the Pueblo Indians in 1680 against the Spanish rulers of New Mexico.

49   Blake, Gladys. Sally Goes to Court. New York, London: Appleton-Century, 1937.
        Novel for teenagers set in time of Maximilian.

50   Blanc, Suzanne. The Rose Window. Garden City: Doubleday, 1967.
        Mystery set in San Luis Potosí, involving an American journalist, Mexican police, and revolutionaries.

Blaisdell, Etta Austin. See McDonald, E.A.B.

51 Bodrero, James. Bomba. New York: Random House,
       1939.
          Children's story about a burro.

Bonehill, Ralph. See Stratemeyer, F.

Borton, Elizabeth. See Treviño, E.B.

52 Botsford, Helen Virginia. Ashes of Gold. New York:
       Dodd, Mead, 1942.
          Novel about the enslavement of an Indian village
          and its reaction to the Mexican Revolution.

53 Bourjaily, Vance Nye. Brill among the Ruins. New
       York: Dial, 1970.
          Novel about an American's escape into Mexican
          archaeology.

Bourne, Peter. See Jeffries, G.M.

54 Bowman, Heath, and Stirling Dickinson. Death Is Inci-
       dental: A Story of Revolution. Chicago: Willett
       Clark, 1937.
          Novel about a Mexican town. The author and the
          illustrator visited Mexico; see 610.

55 Bradbury, Ray. Dandelion Wine. Garden City: Double-
       day, 1957; London: R. Hart-Davis, 1957.
          Section of the novel concerns a telephone call to
          Mexico City.

56 _____. Dark Carnival. Sauk City, Wis.: Arkham
       House, 1947; London: H. Hamilton, 1948.
          "The Next in Line" (short story); reprinted in The
          October Country, 1955: death of an American wom-
          an in Guanajuato. The American author visited
          Mexico in the late 1940's; the celebration of the
          Day of the Dead made a profound impression on
          him (see 59).

57 _____. The Golden Apples of the Sun. Garden City:
       Doubleday, 1953; London: R. Hart-Davis, 1953.
          "Sun and Shadow" (short story): a poor Mexican's
          successful put-down of an American photographer.

58 _____. The Illustrated Man. New York: Doubleday, 1951; London: R. Hart-Davis, 1952.
"The Highway" and "The Fox and the Forest" (short stories): science fiction.

59 _____. The Machineries of Joy. London: R. Hart-Davis, 1964; New York: Simon & Schuster, 1964.
"El Día de Muerte" and "The Life Work of Juan Díaz" (short stories): celebration of the Day of the Dead and another story (see 56) about the mummies of Guanajuato.

60 Brady, Cyrus Townsend. In the War with Mexico: A Midshipman's Adventures on Ship and Shore. New York: Scribner's, 1903.

61 Brand, Anna. Thunder before Seven. New York: Doubleday, Doran, 1941.
Novel about the Texas secession.

62 Brand, Charles Neville (pseud. Charles Lorne). Nocturne in Sunlight. London: J. Lane, 1937. Mexican Masquerade. New York: Dodge, 1938.
Novel about a French painter and an American dancer during the time of Maximilian.

Brand, Max. See Faust, F.S.

63 Brandeis, Madeline Frank. The Little Mexican Donkey Boy. New York: Grosset & Dunlap, 1931.
Children's story.

Brandel, Marc. See Beresford, M.

64 Brautigan, Richard. The Abortion: An Historical Romance, 1966. New York: Simon & Schuster, 1971; London: Cape, 1972.
Last part of the novel sees two California hipsters in Tijuana.

65 Breckenfeld, Vivian Gurney (pseud. Vivian Breck). Maggie. Garden City: Doubleday, 1954.
Novel of an American woman married to a British mining engineer in the mountains of Mexico.

66 Brenner, Anita. The Boy Who Could Do Anything, & Other Mexican Folk Tales. New York: W.R. Scott, 1942.

Folk legends retold for young people; one was published separately as Dumb Juan & the Bandits, 1957. The author was born in Mexico of American parents and lived most of her life there.

67 _____ . A Hero by Mistake. New York: W.R. Scott, 1953.
    Children's story about a Mexican woodchopper.

68 _____ . The Timid Ghost, or What Would You Do with a Sackful of Gold? New York: W.R. Scott, 1966.

69 Brenner, Leah. An Artist Grows Up in Mexico. New York: Beechhurst, 1953.

70 Brereton, Frederick Sadlier. Roger the Bold: A Tale of the Conquest of Mexico. New York, London: Blackie, 1906.

Bronson, Wilfred S. See Coatsworth, E.J.

71 Brown, Harry Peter M'Nab. A Quiet Place to Work. New York: Knopf, 1968.
    Novel of the expatriate scene, centering around an American writer.

72 Brown, J.P.S. Jim Kane. New York: Dial, 1970.
    Western.

73 Bryan, Catherine, and Mabra Madden. The Cactus Fence. New York: Macmillan, 1943.
    Folk tales retold for children.

74 _____ . Pito's House: A Mexican Folk Tale. New York: Macmillan, 1943.

75 Bulla, Clyde Robert. The Poppy Seeds. New York: Crowell, 1955.
    Children's story about a Mexican boy.

76 Burbank, Addison, and Covelle Newcomb. Narizona's Holiday. New York: Longmans, Green, 1946.
    Children's story about a coati and a Mexican boy.

77 Burr, Anna Robeson Brown. The Golden Quicksand: A Novel of Santa Fé. New York: Appleton-Century, 1936.

Novel about an American's search for his brother
during the Mexican-American War.

78 Burroughs, Edgar Rice. The Mucker. London: Methuen,
1921; New York: Grosset & Dunlap, 1921.
Second half of the novel concerns adventures in the
northwestern deserts.

79 Burroughs, William Seward. Naked Lunch. Paris:
Olympia, 1959; New York: Grove, 1962; London:
J. Calder, 1964.
Much of this experimental novel grew out of the
American author's experiences with drugs in Mexi-
co. See 635.

80 _____. The Soft Machine. Paris: Olympia, 1961;
New York: Grove, 1966; London: Calder & Boyars,
1968.
One chapter especially, "The Mayan Caper," deals
with the Maya religion as a system of thought con-
trol.

81 Butka, Hersel Eugene. Mexico through the Eyes of Poet
and Artist. New York: Exposition, 1948.

82 Butler, Edward Crompton. Our Little Mexican Cousin.
Boston: L.C. Page, 1905.
Children's story.

83 Bynner, Witter. Against the Cold. New York: Knopf,
1940.
"Mexican Moon" and "The Mummies of Guanajuato"
(poems).

84 _____. Caravan. New York: Knopf, 1925.
Contains a poem about D.H. Lawrence and one
about Mexico.

85 _____. Indian Earth. New York: Knopf, 1929.
"Prologue" and CHAPALA POEMS. The American
poet first visited Mexico with the D.H. Lawrences
in 1923 (see 638); thereafter he kept a home at
Chapala.

86 Cain, James Mallahan. Serenade. New York: Knopf,
1937; London: J. Cape, 1938.
Novel about the tragedy of an opera singer.

87 Calder-Marshall, Arthur. The Way to Santiago. London: J. Cape, 1940; New York: Reynal & Hitchcock, 1940.
Novel about intrigue at the beginning of World War II. The British writer lived in Mexico.

88 Cameron, Margaret. The Pretender Person. New York, London: Harper, 1911.
Romance about an American woman's involvement by letters with a Mexican.

89 Campbell, Camilla. Star Mountain, and Other Legends of Mexico. New York, London: McGraw, Hill, 1946.
Legends retold for young people.

90 Campbell, Frances W. Men of the Enchantress. Indianapolis: Bobbs-Merrill, 1946.

Carroll, Richard. See Mason, G.

Cavanna, Betty. See Headley, E.C.

91 Chamberlain, George Agnew. Not All the King's Horses. Indianapolis: Bobbs-Merrill, 1919.
Novel about the life of two American mining engineers and their destruction during the Mexican Revolution. The American author was consul-general in Mexico City; see 659.

92 _____. Under Pressure. Indianapolis: Bobbs-Merrill, 1936.
Novel about an American girl's adventurous return to Mexico, where her mother had been slain by bandits.

93 Chambers, María Cristina Mena. Boy Heroes of Chapultepec: A Story of the Mexican War. Philadelphia: Winston, 1953.
Novel for young readers.

94 _____. The Two Eagles. London, New York: Oxford University Pr., 1943.
Novel for teenagers about the visit of an American family, wealthy from copper concessions, to a Mexican governor. The Mexican-born author lived in the United States.

95   Chambers, Robert William. Gitana. New York, Lon-
     don: D. Appleton, 1931.
         Romance of the Mexican-American War.

96   Clagett, John. Cradle of the Sun. New York: Crown,
     1952.
         Romance about a Spanish soldier of the 16th cen-
         tury.

97   Clarke, Laurence. South of the Rio Grande. New York:
     Macaulay, 1924.
         Novel about an American, working for the British
         government, who attempts to gain the papers grant-
         ing an oil concession.

98   Clemens, Jeremiah. Bernard Lile: An Historical
     Romance Embracing the Periods of the Texas Revolu-
     tion and the Mexican War. Philadelphia: J.B. Lip-
     pincott, 1856.

99   Coatsworth, Elizabeth Jane. The Noble Doll. New
     York: Viking, 1961.
         Children's story about a Mexican girl during the
         Christmas season.

100 _____ (pseud. Wilfred S. Bronson). Tonio and the
     Stranger: A Mexican Adventure. New York: Grosset
     & Dunlap, 1941.
         Story for young readers.

101 Coleman, Eleanor S. The Cross and the Sword of
     Cortes. New York: Simon & Schuster, 1968.

102 Collins, Clarissa W. Mexican Vignettes. New York:
     Snellgrove, 1938.
         Poetry.

103 Collin-Smith, Joyce. Jeremy Craven. London: Hodder
     & Stoughton, 1958; Boston: Houghton Mifflin, 1959.
         Novel about an English boy's adventures during the
         Mexican Revolution.

104 Comfort, Will Levington. Somewhere South in Sonora.
     Boston: Houghton Mifflin, 1925.
         Novel about an American's search for a missing
         man.

105   Coolidge, Dane. <u>Wolf's Candle.</u> New York: E.P.
      Dutton, 1935; London: Skeffington, 1936.
      Novel about the adventures of an American man and
      a Spanish woman during the Mexican Revolution.

106   Corso, Gregory. <u>Gasoline.</u> San Francisco: City
      Lights, 1958.
      "Mexican Impressions," "Sun," and "Puma in
      Chapultepec Zoo" (poems). The author, in company
      with Allen Ginsberg, visited Jack Kerouac in Mexi-
      co City in 1956; see 253.

107   Coyner, David Holmes. <u>The Lost Trappers: A Collec-
      tion of Interesting Scenes and Events in the Rocky
      Mountains; Together with a Short Description of Cali-
      fornia.</u> Cincinnati: J.A. & U.P. James, 1847.
      Although published as truth, much of this work is
      apparently fiction.

108   Crane, (Harold) Hart. <u>The Collected Poems,</u> ed. Waldo
      David Frank. New York: Liveright, 1933; London:
      Boriswood, 1938.
      "The Broken Tower," "The Sad Indian," "The Cir-
      cumstance," "Purgatorio," and "Havana Rose"
      (poems). The American poet lived in Mexico City
      and Taxco 1931-1932; see 677.

109   Crane, Stephen. <u>Last Words.</u> London: Digby, Long,
      1902.
      "How the Donkey Lifted the Hills," "The Voice of
      the Mountain," and "The Victory of the Moon"
      (original fables).

110   _____. <u>The Open Boat, and Other Tales of Adven-
      ture.</u> New York: Doubleday & McClure, 1898. <u>The
      Open Boat, and Other Stories.</u> London: W. Heine-
      mann, 1898.
      "The Wise Men," "The Five White Mice," and
      "Horses--One Dash" (short stories): two comedies
      of the Anglo-American colony in Mexico City and
      an American's encounter with Mexican bandits in
      southern Mexico. These were based on the Amer-
      ican author's own experiences in 1895; see 678.

111   Crary, Margaret. <u>Mexican Whirlwind.</u> New York:
      Washburn, 1969.

112 Credle, Ellis. My Pet Peepelo. New York: Oxford
University, 1948.
Children's story about a Mexican boy and his pet
turkey.

113 _____. Pepe and the Parrot. New York: T. Nelson, 1937.
Children's story about a dog and his hatred of the
parrot.

114 Creeley, Robert. Pieces. New York: Scribner's,
1969.
"Mazatlan: Sea" (poem).

115 Culp, John Hewett. The Men of Gonzales. New York:
W. Sloan, 1960.
Novel about the Texas secession.

116 Curtis, Edith Roelker. Mexican Romance. Philadelphia: Dorrance, 1969.

117 Curtis, Newton Mallory. The Vidette, or The Girl of
the Robber's Pass: A Tale of the Mexican War. New
York: Williams, 1848.

118 Dagnall, John Malone. The Mexican, or Love and
Land; Founded on the Invasion of Maximilian. New
York: American News, 1868.

119 Dahlberg, Edward. Cipango's Hinder Door. Austin:
University of Texas, 1965.
The volume contains several poems reflecting the
American author's interest in Indian mythology.
He lived in Mexico City in the late 1930's.

120 Davis, Edwin Adams. Of the Night Wind's Telling:
Legends from the Valley of Mexico. Norman: Uni-
versity of Oklahoma, 1946.
The author spent several months in Mexico.

121 Decatur, Dorothy Durbin. Two Young Americans in
Mexico. New York: D.C. Heath, 1938.
Children's story about travel.

122 De la Rhue, Treviño. Spanish Trails to California.
Caldwell, Id.: Caxton, 1937.

Novel about Spanish immigration into the (now) American Southwest, set in 1760. The story was based on tales given the author by Mexican-American cowboys.

Dennis, Patrick. See Tanner, E.E.

123 Detzer, Karl William. Contrabando. Indianapolis: Bobbs-Merrill, 1936; London: Wright & Brown, 1938. Novel about smuggling along the Mexican border.

124 Deutsch, Hermann Bacher. The Wedge: A Novel of Mexico. New York: F.A. Stokes, 1935.

Dickinson, Stirling. See Bowman, H.

125 Dill, Margaret. The Story of Burro Big Ears. Los Angeles: Suttonhouse, 1935. Children's story.

126 Dix, Beulah Marie. Hands Off! New York: Macmillan, 1919; London: E. Nash, 1920. Novel about an American's involvement in a revenge case.

127 Dobie, James Frank. Apache Gold & Yaqui Silver. Boston: Little, Brown, 1939.

128 _____. Coronado's Children: Tales of Lost Mines and Buried Treasure of the Southwest. New York: Grosset & Dunlap, 1930. Legends [127-8]. The American author made several pack-trips between 1928 and 1933 to isolated sections of northern Mexico; see 694-695.

129 Dos Passos, John Roderigo. The 42nd Parallel. New York: Harper, 1930. The Forty Second Parallel. London: Constable, 1930. "Mac" section concerns an American Wobbly's involvement in the Mexican Revolution. The American author visited Mexico in 1926; see 699.

130 Downing, Todd. The Last Trumpet: Murder in a Mexican Bull Ring. Garden City: Doubleday-Doran, 1937; London: Methuen, 1938.

131 _____. Murder on the Tropic. Garden City: Doubleday-Doran, 1935; London: Methuen, 1936.

132 _____ . Night over Mexico. Garden City: Doubleday-Doran, 1937; London: Methuen, 1938.

133 _____ . Vultures in the Sky. Garden City: Doubleday-Doran, 1935; London: Methuen, 1936.
Mysteries [130-3]. The author lived in Mexico; see
700.

134 Drago, Harry Sinclair. Suzanna: A Romance of Early
California. New York: Macaulay, 1922; London:
Hutchinson, 1924.
Novel about the complications of love among Mexi-
cans of several classes.

135 _____ (pseud. Bliss Lomax). Gringo Gunfire. New
York: Doubleday, Doran, 1940.
Western.

136 Duffus, Robert Luther. Jornada. London: Hutchinson,
1935; New York: Covici, Friede, 1935.
Romance set during the Mexican-American War.

137 Duggan, Janie Prichard. A Mexican Ranch, or Beauty
for Ashes. Philadelphia: American Baptist, 1894.

138 _____ . The Señora's Granddaughters: A Tale of
Modern Mexico. London: Baptist Tract & Book,
1898; Philadelphia: American Baptist, 1898.

139 Durfee, Burr, Helen McMorris, and John McMorris.
Mateo and Lolita. Boston: Houghton Mifflin, 1939.
Children's story.

140 Duval, John Crittenden. Early Times in Texas. Austin:
H. P. N. Gammel, 1892.
Based closely on fact, it is questionable whether
this is fiction or memoirs.

Dwyer, Eileen. See Reid, T. M. E. B.

141 Eliot, Frances. Pablo's Pipes. New York: E. P. Dutton, 1936.
Children's story.

142 Ellerbe, Rose Lucile. Ropes of Sand. Hollywood:
D. G. Fischer, 1925.

143 _____ . Tales of California Yesterdays. Los Angel-
      es: W.J. Potter, 1916.

144 Ets, Marie Hall, and Aurora Labastida. Nine Days to
      Christmas. New York: Viking, 1959.
      Children's story about a Mexican girl at Christmas.

145 Eyster, Warren. The Goblins of Eros. London: V.
      Gollancz, 1957; New York: Random House, 1957.
      Novel about decadence in a village.

146 Faust, Frederick Schiller (pseud. Max Brand). South
      of Rio Grande. New York: Dodd, Mead, 1936; Lon-
      don: Hodder & Stoughton, 1937.
      Western.

147 Ferrer, Melchor G. (with Jean Charlot). Tito's Hats.
      New York: Garden City, 1940.
      Children's story about a Mexican boy's first hair-
      cut.

148 Ficke, Arthur Davison. Mrs. Morton of Mexico. New
      York: Reynal & Hitchcock, 1939.
      Novel about the life of an Englishwoman in a remote
      village.

      Field, Matthew C. Mott. See 729.

      Fierro Blanco, Antonio de. See Nordhoff, W.

149 Fifield, William. The Sign of Taurus. London: Weiden-
      feld & Nicolson, 1959; New York: Holt, Rinehart &
      Winston, 1960.
      Novel about a Polish Jewish fortune teller and her
      relationship with an Italian ex-Fascist.

150 Flack, Marjorie, and Karl Larsson. Pedro. New
      York: Macmillan, 1940.
      Children's story in which a Mexican boy saves the
      life of an American boy at a rodeo.

151 Flandrau, Charles Macomb. Prejudices. New York,
      London: D. Appleton, 1911.
      "Wanderlust" (short story): tragedy of two Amer-
      ican sailors stranded in Veracruz. The American
      author visited Mexico many times; see 724-725.

152   Flint, Timothy. Francis Berrian, or The Mexican Pa-
      triot. Philadelphia: 1826; London: 1834.
          First American novel set (partly) in Mexico. The
      author never visited the country (but see 968).

153   Flora, James. The Fabulous Firework Family. New
      York: Harcourt, Brace, 1955.
          Children's story.

154   Fosdick, William Whiteman. Malmiztic the Toltec, and
      The Cavaliers of the Cross. Cincinnati: 1851.

155   Foster, Joseph O'Kane. The Great Montezuma. Ranchos
      de Taos: Ranchos, 1940.
          Film script.

156   _____. Street of Barefoot Lovers. New York:
      Duell, Sloan & Pearce, 1953.
          Novel about the life of the poor in Mexico City.

157   Foulke, William Dudley. Maya: A Drama. New York:
      Cosmopolitan, 1911.

158   _____. Maya: A Story of Yucatan. New York,
      London: G. P. Putnam's, 1900.
          The author visited Mexico; see 734-735.

159   Fox, Frances Margaret. Carlota: A Story of the San
      Gabriel Mission. Boston: L. C. Page, 1908.

160   Francis, Francis Jr. Wild Rose: A Tale of the Mexi-
      can Frontier. New York, London: Macmillan, 1895.

161   Frings, Ketti. Hold Back the Dawn. New York: Duell,
      Sloan & Pearce, 1940.
          Novel about immigrants waiting in Tijuana to enter
      California. The novel was based on the author's
      own experience.

162   Gaines, Ruth Louise. Little Light (Lucita): A Child's
      Story of Old Mexico. Chicago: Rand McNally, 1913.

163   _____, and Georgia Willis Read. The Village Shield:
      A Story of Mexico. New York: E. P. Dutton, 1917.
          Children's story of Indians.

164 Ganilh, Anthony. Mexico versus Texas: A Descriptive
     Novel, Most of the Characters of Which Consist of
     Living Persons; by a Texian. Philadelphia: N. Sieg-
     fried, 1838.

165 Garrett, Helen. Angelo, the Naughty One. New York:
     Viking, 1944.
         Children's story about a Mexican boy on the day of
     his sister's wedding.

166 Garrison, Aletheia. Impressions of Mexico: Verse.
     New York: R. W. Kelly, 1937.

167 Garthwaite, Marion. Mario: A Mexican Boy's Adven-
     ture. Garden City: Doubleday, 1960.
         Novel for young readers about a Mexican boy kid-
     napped in Tijuana and taken into the United States
     to work.

168 Gavin, Catherine Irvine. The Cactus and the Crown.
     Garden City: Doubleday, 1962; London: Hodder &
     Stoughton, 1962.
         Romance about Americans and French during the
     time of Maximilian.

169 Gay, Zhenya, and Jan Gay. Pancho and His Burro.
     New York: W. Morrow, 1930.
         Children's story about a Mexican boy and a girl.

170 Gellhorn, Martha. The Lowest Trees Have Tops. New
     York: Dodd, Mead, 1969.
         Novel about expatriates.

171 Gerard (Laszowska), Emily, and Dorothea Gerard
     Longard de Longgarde (pseud. E. D. Gerard). Reata,
     or What's in a Name. Edinburgh, London: W. Black-
     wood, 1880; New York: G. Munro, 1880.

172 Gerould, Katherine Fullerton. Conquistador. New York:
     Scribner's, 1923. Conquistador, and Other Stories.
     London: G. G. Harrap, 1924.
         Novel about an American engineer, son of a Mexi-
     can mother, who hunts up his family hacienda and
     subsequently inherits it, during the days of Fran-
     cisco Villa (Mexican Revolution).

173 Gerson, Noel Bertram. The Golden Eagle. Garden
     City: Doubleday, 1953; London: Transworld, 1953.

Romance set during the Mexican-American War.

174   Gill, Tom. Death Rides the Mesa. London: W. Col-
      lins, 1934; New York: Farrar & Rinehart, 1934.
      Western, set in northern Mexico.

175   Ginsberg, Allen. Reality Sandwiches, 1953-60. San
      Francisco: City Lights, 1963.
      "Siesta in Xbalba, and Return to the States" (poems):
      survey of Indian ruins in Yucatán and a travelogue,
      based on the American poet's visit in 1954.

176   Giusti, Arndt. An Artist Passes. London: Chatto &
      Windus, 1929; New York: Dodd, Mead, 1929.
      Novel about the rise and fall of a Mexican peasant,
      turned cosmopolitan artist because of an American
      woman.

      Goertz, Arthémise. See 781.

177   Goldsmith, Martin M. The Miraculous Fish of Domingo
      Gonzales. New York: Norton, 1950; London: Ham-
      mond, Hammond, 1951.
      Satiric novel about a fishing village invaded by
      American commerce.

      Gooch, Fanny Chambers. See Iglehart, F.C.G.

178   Goodman, Paul. Homespun of Oatmeal Gray. New
      York: Random House, 1970.
      "An Amate Tree" (poem). The American author
      visited CIDOC in Cuernavaca.

179   Goodspeed, Bernice I. Mexican Tales: A Compilation
      of Mexican Stories and Legends.... México: Cvltvra,
      1937.

180   _____. Paricutín. México: American Book &
      Print, 1945.

181   Gorman, Herbert Sherman. The Breast of the Dove.
      New York: Rinehart, 1950.
      Romance set in the time of Maximilian.

182   _____. The Cry of Dolores. New York, Toronto:
      Rinehart, 1948.

Novel about the beginning of the War for Independence, centering around Father Miguel Hidalgo.

183   . The Wine of San Lorenzo. New York: Farrar & Rinehart, 1945; London: Cassell, 1948.
Novel about an American boy, raised as a Mexican, in the Mexican-American War.

184 Graham, Carroll. Border Town. New York: Vanguard, 1934.
Novel about the adventures of a murderer in Mexicali.

185 Graham, Gabriela Cunninghame. The Christ of Toro, and Other Stories. London: E. Nash, 1908.
"The Waggon-Train" (short story): account of a trek from Mexico City to Texas, based on actual experience in 1880 (see 186). The author was born in Chili.

186 Graham, Robert Bontine Cunninghame. Thirteen Stories. London: W. Heinemann, 1900.
"A Hegira" (short story): account based on the same experience as his wife's (see 185). The author was English.

187 Graham, Sarah Melissa Cary Downing. The Toltec Savior: A Historical Romance of Ancient Mexico. New York: G.W. Dillingham, 1901.

188 Grant, Robert. Shorn! London: J. Murray, 1927; New York: E.P. Dutton, 1928.
Novel about the punishment of a foreigner financially backing revolts.

189 Grayson, Charles. Flight South. New York: Macaulay, 1935.
Novel about a twin brother and sister, American ne'er-do-wells.

190 Greene, Graham. Nineteen Stories. London: W. Heinemann, 1945; New York: Viking, 1949.
"Across the Bridge" (short story); reprinted in Twenty-One Stories, 1954: tragi-comedy of a British embezzler in Nuevo Laredo.

191   . The Power and the Glory. London: W. Heinemann, 1940. The Labyrinthe Ways. New York:

Viking, 1940.
The original title was used for later American
editions. Novel about religious persecution in
southern Mexico, centering around a "whiskey"
priest and a police lieutenant. The English author
visited Mexico in 1938; see 781.

192   Gregory, Jackson. Captain Cavalier. London: Hodder
      & Stoughton, 1927; New York: Scribner's, 1927.
      Romance about a Virginia pirate and a Spanish lady
      of California.

193   _____. Sentinel of the Desert. London: Hodder &
      Stoughton, 1929; New York: Dodd, Mead, 1929.
      Novel of adventure.

194   _____ (pseud. Quién Sabe). Daughter of the Sun: A
      Tale of Adventure. New York: Scribner's, 1921;
      London: Hodder & Stoughton, 1923.

195   Grey, Zane. Desert Gold: A Romance of the Border.
      New York, London: Harper, 1913; London: T. Nel-
      son, 1919.
      Western.

196   _____. Ken Ward in the Jungle: Thrilling Adven-
      tures in Tropical Wilds. New York, London: Harper,
      1912; London: T. Nelson, 1919.
      Novel for teenagers set in the Sierra west of
      Tampico. The American author had explored this
      region in 1911; see 785.

197   Grogan, Gerald. William Pollok, and Other Tales.
      London, New York: J. Lane, 1919.

198   Gunter, Archibald Clavering. The Spy Company: A
      Story of the Mexican War. New York: Home, 1902;
      London: Ward, Lock, 1903.

199   Hader, Berta Hoerner, and Elmer Stanley Hader. The
      Story of Pancho and the Bull with the Crooked Tail.
      New York: Macmillan, 1942; London: R. Hale, 1946.
      Children's story about a Mexican boy.

200   Haggard, Henry Rider. Heart of the World. New York:
      Longmans, Green, 1895; London: Longmans, 1896.

Romance about an Englishman and an Indian of
royal blood finding a lost Maya civilization as of
old. The English author visited Mexico in 1891;
see 792.

201 _____ . Montezuma's Daughter. London: Longmans,
1893; New York: Longmans, Green, 1893.
Romance of an Englishman's participation in the
Spanish Conquest on the side of the Aztecs.

202 Hale, Edward Everett, and Susan Hale. A Family
Flight through Mexico. Boston: D. Lothrop, 1886.
Children's story of travel.

203 Hamby, William Henry. The Ranch of the Thorn: An
Adventure Story. London: Hutchinson, 1924; New
York: Chelsea, 1924.

204 Hancock, Harrie Irving. Dave Darrin at Vera Cruz, or
Fighting with the U.S. Navy in Mexico. Philadelphia:
H. Altemus, 1914.
Novel for teenagers based on the occupation of the
same year.

205 Hanley, May Carr. Stories from Mañana Land. Mountain View, Calif.: Pacific, 1922.
The author was in mission work; see 801.

206 Harper, Theodore Acland, and Winifred Harper. Forgotten Gods. Garden City: Doubleday, Doran, 1929.

207 Harrison, Harry. Captive Universe. New York: Putnam, 1969; London: Faber & Faber, 1970.
Science fiction, using Aztec mythology.

208 Hawk, Alex. Mexican Standoff. New York: Paperback
Library, 1970.
Western.

209 Hawthorne, Hildegarde. The Secret of Rancho de Sol:
A Story of Old California. New York, London: D.
Appleton, 1931.
Mystery for teenagers.

210 Hayden, Robert Earl. Selected Poems. New York:
October House, 1966.

AN INFERENCE OF MEXICO (poems).   The American poet was in Mexico 1954-1955.

211   Hays, Hoffman Reynolds.   The Takers of the City.   New
York: Reynal & Hitchcock, 1946; London: S. Low,
Marston, 1947.
Romance of the 16th century, centering about Fa-
ther Bartolomé de las Casas.

212   Headley, Elizabeth Cavanna (Betty Cavanna).   Carlos of
Mexico.   London: Chatto & Windus, 1964; New York:
F. Watts, 1964.
Novel for teenagers.

213   Helm, MacKinley.   Fray Junípero Serra, the Great
Walker.   Stanford: Stanford University, 1956.
Verse drama of California of the 18th century.

214   _____.   A Matter of Love, and Other Baroque Tales
of the Provinces.   New York, London: Harper, 1946.
A Month of Sundays, and Other Baroque Tales of the
Provinces.   London: Harvill, 1949.
Short stories about life in a town as seen by an
American visitor.   The American author lived in
Mexico.

215   Helprin, Benjamin.   Pagan Cross: A Romance of Pre-
Conquest Yucatan.   Roslyn, N.Y.:   Raiben, 1938.

216   Hemingway, Ernest.   Winner Take Nothing.   New York:
Scribner's, 1933; London: J. Cape, 1934.
"The Mother of a Queen" (short story):   Problems
of a homosexual bullfighter, based on an anecdote
told the American author (who did not visit Mexico
until the 1940's).

217   Henderson, James Leal.   Whirlpool.   New York:
Prentice-Hall, 1947.
Novel of lost people in a small village on the Pa-
cific coast.

Henry, O.   See Porter, W.S.

218   Henty, George Alfred.   By Right of Conquest, or With
Cortez in Mexico.   London: Blackie, 1891; New York:
A.L. Burt, 189-.

219 Hergesheimer, Joseph. Tampico. New York: Knopf,
1926; London: W. Heinemann, 1927.
Novel about the return of an American oilman to
the fields. The American author visited Mexico in
1925.

220 Hersch, Virginia Davis. The Seven Cities of Gold.
New York: Duell, Sloan & Pearce, 1946.
Romance about the second expedition of Francisco
Vázquez de Coronado.

221 Highsmith, Patricia. A Game for the Living. New
York: Harper, 1958; London: Heinemann, 1959.
Mystery.

222 Hirschfeld, Burt. Acapulco. New York: Arbor House,
1971.

223 Hobart, Alice Tisdale Nourse. The Peacock Sheds His
Tail. Indianapolis: Bobbs-Merrill, 1945; London:
Cassell, 1946.
Novel about social changes and their effect on an
aristocratic family in Mexico City.

224 Hoffman, Gloria. Primitivo and His Dog. New York:
E. P. Dutton, 1949.
Children's story.

225 Hoffman, Nathan. Maximilian's Phantom Crown. Los
Angeles: Wetzel, 1938.

226 Hogner, Dorothy Childs. The Education of a Burro.
New York: T. Nelson, 1936.
Children's story about Mexican peasants. The
American author visited Mexico; see 818.

227 _____. Pancho. New York: T. Nelson, 1938.
Children's story.

228 Holden, Curry. Hill of the Rooster. New York: Holt,
1956.
Novel about the Yaqui Indians (sometime after World
War I).

229 Holton (Neff), Priscilla. Chuck Martinez. New York,
Toronto: Longmans, Green, 1940.

Novel for teenagers about the return of a Mexican
boy, reared as an American, to his father.

230   Hope, Laura Lee. The Bobbsey Twins in Mexico. New
York: Grosset & Dunlap, 1947.
Children's story about a trip to Mexico City.

231   Hough, Emerson. Mother of Gold. New York, London:
D. Appleton, 1924.
Novel about a lost mine and love between various
Americans, set near the border.

232   Household, Geoffrey. The Third Hour. London: Chatto
& Windus, 1937; Boston: Little, Brown, 1938.
Novel about revolution, buried treasure, and a
Utopian scheme, involving a Mexican and an Amer-
ican.

233   Hughes, (James) Langston. The Weary Blues. New
York: Knopf, 1926.
"Mexican Market Woman" (poem).   The American
author lived in Toluca 1919-1921; see 826 (also
827).

Hunt, Helen Maria. See Jackson, H. M. H.

234   Hunt, Howard. Maelstrom. New York: Farrar,
Straus, 1948.
Novel of adventure involving three expatriates.

235   Huxley, Aldous Leonard. Eyeless in Gaza. London:
Chatto & Windus, 1936; New York: Harper, 1936.
Section of the novel concerns a hazardous trip
through southern Mexico.   The English author
visited the area in 1933; see 832.

236   Iglehart, Fanny Chambers Gooch. The Boy Captive of
the Texas Mier Expedition. Rev. ed. San Antonio:
J. R. Wood, 1909.
Novel for teenagers about the Texas secession.
See also 833.

237   Ingraham, Joseph Holt. Montezuma the Serf, or The
Revolt of the Mexitili: A Tale of the Last Days of
the Aztec Dynasty. Boston: H. L. Williams, 1845.

238 Jackson, Helen Maria Hunt. Ramona. Boston: Rob-
     erts, 1884; London, Edinburgh: Macmillan, 1884.
     Romance of California.

239 Jackson, Joseph Henry. The Christmas Flower. New
     York: Harcourt, Brace, 1951.
          Short story about a Christmas miracle. The author
     visited Mexico; see 835.

240 Janvier, Thomas Allibone. The Aztec Treasure-House:
     A Romance of Contemporaneous Antiquity. New York:
     Harper, 1890; London: S. Low, 1891.

241   . Color Studies, and A Mexican Campaign.
     New York: Scribner's, 1891.
          Short story.

242   . Legends of the City of Mexico. New York,
     London: Harper, 1910.

243   . Stories of Old New Spain. London: Osgood
     & McIlvaine, 1891; New York: D. Appleton, 1891.

244 Jarrell, Randall. The Complete Poems. New York:
     Farrar, Straus & Giroux, 1969.
          "An Indian Market in Mexico" (poem). The Amer-
     ican poet visited Mexico in 1942.

245 Jebb, Bertha (Mrs. J. Gladwyn Jebb). Some Unconven-
     tional People. Boston: Roberts, 1895; Edinburgh,
     London: Blackwood, 1896.
          Short stories. The author lived in Mexico; see
     842.

246 Jeffries, Graham Montague (pseud. Peter Bourne).
     Flames of Empire. New York: Putnam's, 1949.
          Tragic romance of an American in Maximilian's
     service.

247 Jennings, John Edward. Shadows in the Dust. Boston:
     Little, Brown, 1955.
          Novel about the Santa Fe uprising of 1837.

248 Johnston, Sue Mildred Lee (pseud.). Overlord. New
     York: Scribner's, 1933.
          Novel about a Mexican restored to his rightful posi-
     tion.

249 Jolly, Andrew. Lie Down in Me. New York: Crown, 1970.
     Novel about a Mexican's pilgrimage to bury his Yaqui Indian wife.

250 Kauffmann, Stanley. The Hidden Hero. New York, Toronto: Rinehart, 1949; London: Collins, 1951.
     Novel about an American couple.

251 Keene, Day. Acapulco G. P. O. New York: 1967.

252 Kemp, Lysander. The Conquest, and Other Poems from Spanish America. Austin: University of Texas, 1970.
     "In Mexico," "Metzli," "The Stars of Heaven," "Catarino Maravillas," "The Death of Refugio Godoy," and "The Conquest" (poems). The American author lived some time in Mexico.

253 Kerouac, Jack (Jean Louis Lebris de Kerouac). Desolation Angels. New York: Coward-McCann, 1965.
     Long section of the picaresque novel grew out of the American author's experiences in Mexico City in 1956.

254 _____. Mexico City Blues. New York: Grove, 1959.
     Poems improvised there in 1955.

255 _____. On the Road. New York: Viking, 1957; London: A. Deutsch, 1958.
     End of the picaresque novel concerns the author's trip to Mexico City in 1950.

256 _____. Tristessa. New York: Avon, 1960. Visions of Gerard, and Tristessa. London: A. Deutsch, 1964.
     Novel about a love affair with a Mexican girl, based on events of 1955-1956.

257 _____. Visions of Cody. New York: McGraw-Hill, 1972.
     Section of the novel deals with the same experience as 255. See also 854.

258 Kidwell, Carl. Arrow in the Sun. New York: Viking, 1961.

259 Kirkham, Kate. Sun and Shadow. Atlanta: Banner,
     1936.
        Poems.

260 Knibbs, Henry (or Harry) Herbert. Temescal. Boston:
     Houghton Mifflin, 1925; London: Hutchinson, 1925.
        Novel of romance and adventures during the early
        days of the Mexican Revolution.

261 Knox, Thomas Wallace. The Boy Travellers in Mexi-
     co: Adventures of Two Youths in a Journey to North-
     ern and Central Mexico, Campeachey, Yucatan, with
     a Description of the Republics of Central America....
     New York: Harper, 1890.

262 Kohan, Frances H., and Truda T. Weil. Eagle in the
     Valley. Chicago: Children's, 1951.
        Children's story.

263 Krey, Laura Lettie Smith. On the Long Tide. Boston:
     Houghton Mifflin, 1940.
        Novel partly concerned with the Texas secession.

     Labistida, Aurora. See Ets, M.H.

264 Lampman, Evelyn Sibley. Temple of the Sun: A Boy
     Fights for Montezuma. Garden City: Doubleday,
     1964.
        Novel for young readers.

265   . The Tilted Sombrero. Garden City: Double-
     day, 1966.

     Larsson, Karl. See Flack, M.

266 Lasswell, Mary. Tío Pepe. Boston: Houghton Mifflin,
     1963.

     Laszowska, Emily Gerard. See Gerard, E.

267 Lawrence, David Herbert. Phoenix: The Posthumous
     Papers..., ed. Edward David McDonald. London:
     W. Heinemann, 1936; New York: Viking, 1936.
        "The Flying Fish" (opening of novel): an English-
        man leaves the south of Mexico to return home.
        "Au Revoir, U.S.A." and "See Mexico After, by
        Luis Q." (essays): comparisons of the United

States and Mexico. The English author made three
visits 1923-1925. See also 872-873.

268 _____. The Plumed Serpent (Quetzalcoatl). London:
A. Secker, 1926; New York: Knopf, 1926.
Novel about a British woman's search for meaning,
in which process she encounters an attempt by two
Mexicans to resurrect the Aztec religion.

269 _____. The Woman Who Rode Away, and Other
Stories. London: M. Secker, 1928; New York:
Knopf, 1928.
"The Woman Who Rode Away" and "None of That"
(short stories): a woman finds her death at the
hands of an Indian tribe but in the process comes
to understand the meaning of life; another finds a
meaningless death through the machinations of a
bullfighter.

270 Lay, Marion. Wooden Saddles: The Adventures of a
Mexican Boy in His Own Land. New York: W. Morrow, 1939.
Novel for young readers about a boy who runs
away from his gypsy captors and lives among villagers.

271 Lea, Tom. The Brave Bulls. Boston: Little, Brown,
1949; London: W. Heinemann, 1950.
Novel about a bullfighter.

272 _____. The Hands of Cantú. Boston: Little, Brown,
1964; London: Hammond, Hammond, 1964.
Romance about a 16th-century Spanish horsetrainer
and his expedition against rustlers, narrated by a
young boy.

273 _____. The Wonderful Country. Boston: Little,
Brown, 1952; London: W. Heinemann, 1953.
Novel about a Texan who lived many years in Mexi-
co coming back to El Paso; the time is the 1880's.

274 Lee, Melicent Humason. Marcos, a Mountain Boy of
Mexico. Chicago: A. Whitman, 1937.
Story for young readers about a boy finding work
in Oaxaca.

275 _____. Pablo and Petra: A Boy and Girl of Mexico.
New York: Crowell, 1934.

Children's story about two children taking their
wares to market in Oaxaca.

276 Leonard, Elsmore. The Bounty Hunters. Boston:
       Houghton Mifflin, 1954.
              Novel of adventure, set in the 19th century, about
              the chase after an Apache chief.

277 Le Plongeon, Alice Dixon. Queen Moo's Talisman:
       The Fall of the Maya Empire. London: K. Paul,
       1902; New York: Eckler, 1902.
              Poem, based upon the myth of Mu. See 882.

278 Levertov, Denise. Here and Now. San Francisco:
       City Lights, 1957.
              "Tomatlán" (variations on a poem). The British-
              born poet lived in Guadalajara with her American
              husband 1956-1958.

279 _____. The Jacob's Ladder. New York: New Di-
       rections, 1961; London: J. Cape, 1965.
              FIVE POEMS FROM MEXICO (poems).

280 _____. Overland to the Islands. Highlands, N.C.:
       J. Williams, 1958.
              "Overland to the Islands," "A Supermarket in
              Guadalajara, Mexico," "Scenes from the Life of
              the Peppertrees," "Pure Products," "Broken
              Glass," "Sunday Afternoon," and "The Whirlwind"
              (poems); some were reprinted in 279.

281 _____. The Sorrow Dance. New York: New Direc-
       tions, 1966.
              "As It Happens" (poem).

282 _____. With Eyes at the Back of Our Heads. New
       York: New Directions, 1959.
              "Xochipilli" and "Triple" (poems).

283 Lewis, Oscar. The Children of Sánchez: Autobiography
       of a Mexican Family. New York: Random House,
       1961; London: Secker & Warburg, 1962.
              Anthropological study of a poor family in Mexico
              City, told in novel form. The American anthro-
              pologist spent many years interviewing families
              there and in Tepoztlán.

284 _____ . A Death in the Sánchez Family. New York:
Random House, 1969.
Similar study, revolving around the death and fu-
neral of an aunt.

285 _____ . Five Families: Mexican Case Studies in the
Culture of Poverty. New York: Basic Books, 1959.
Stories about a typical day in the lives of families
in Mexico City.

286 _____ . Pedro Martínez: A Mexican Peasant and
His Family. London: Secker & Warburg, 1964; New
York: Random House, 1964.
Another anthropological study told in novel form.

287 Lewis, Wells. They Still Say No. New York: Farrar
& Rinehart, 1939.
Novel about a Harvard freshman on summer vaca-
tion.

288 Lide, Alice Alison. Aztec Drums. New York, Toronto:
Longmans, Green, 1938.
Children's story about an Aztec weaver who makes
a feathered robe for Moctezuma.

289 _____ . Princess of Yucatan. New York, Toronto:
Longmans, Green, 1939.
Children's story about the escape of a Maya slave,
to be sacrificed by the Aztecs.

290 Lindop, Audrey Erskine. The Judas Figures. London:
Heinemann, 1956; New York: Appleton-Century-Crofts,
1956.
Novel about the attempts of a priest to rid his village of an outlaw's evil influence, which has con-
tinued even after his death.

291 _____ . The Singer Not the Song. London: Heinemann, 1953; New York: Appleton-Century-Crofts,
1953.
Novel about the fight between a village priest and
an outlaw.

292 Lippard, George. 'Bel of Prairie Eden: A Romance
of Mexico. Boston: Hotchkiss, 1848.

293 _____ . Legends of Mexico: ... The Battles of Taylor.
Philadelphia: T.B. Peterson, 1847.

294   Litten, Frederic Nelson. Pilot of the High Sierras.
        New York: Dodd, Mead, 1937.

295   Lobdell, Helen. Golden Conquest. Boston: Houghton
        Mifflin, 1953.
            Romance for young readers about a Spanish boy and
            an Indian girl during the Conquest.

296   Locke, Charles Otis. The Taste of Infamy: The Ad-
        ventures of John Kilane. New York: Norton, 1960.
        The Taste of Infamy. London: Hutchinson, 1961.
            Novel of revenge, centering around a Texan who
            went after his brother's murderer.

      Lomax, Bliss. See Drago, H.S.

297   London, Jack (John Griffith). The Night Born... New
        York: Century, 1913; London: Mills & Boon, 1916.
            "The Mexican" (short story): a Mexican fighter in
            Los Angeles, working for a junta and recalling his
            childhood in Mexico. The American author did not
            visit Mexico until 1914 (see 887).

298   Long, Haniel. Malinche (Doña Marina). Santa Fe:
        Writers', 1939.

      Longard de Longgarde, Dorothea Gerard. See Gerard,
      E.

299   Longfellow, Henry Wadsworth. In the Harbor...
        Boston: Houghton Mifflin, 1882; London: Routledge,
        1882.
            "The Bells of San Blas" (poem): based on a maga-
            zine article, this was the American poet's last
            work.

300   Lord, David. The Ravager. New York: F. Fell,
        1947.
            Novel about life in a village.

      Lorne, Charles. See Brand, C.N.

301   Lowell, Robert. Notebook 1967-68. New York: Far-
        rar, Straus & Giroux, 1969.
            "Mexico" (poems): episodes from the American
            poet's visit to CIDOC in Cuernavaca.

302 Lowry, (Clarence) Malcolm. Dark as the Grave Where-
     in My Friend Is Laid, ed Douglas Day and Margerie
     Bonner Lowry. New York: New American Library,
     1968; London: J. Cape, 1969.
        Novel based on the English author's 1945-1946 re-
     turn visit to search out an old Mexican friend and
     to verify details for 304. See also 889.

303   . Selected Poems, ed. Earle Birney and
     Margerie Bonner Lowry. San Francisco: City Lights,
     1962.
        THUNDER BEYOND POPOCATEPETL, THE CANTI-
     NAS (poems).

304   . Under the Volcano. London: J. Cape,
     1947; New York: Reynal & Hitchcock, 1947.
        Novel about the last day (November 2, 1938) in the
     life of the drunken British consul-general of a town
     modelled on Cuernavaca (and Oaxaca). The author
     lived in Cuernavaca 1936-1938.

305 Lucas, Cary. Unfinished Business. New York: Simon
     & Schuster, 1947.
        Political mystery involving an American, an Irish-
     Mexican woman, and the FBI.

306 Lyle, Eugene P. Jr. The Missourian. London: W.
     Heinemann, 1905; New York: Doubleday, Page, 1905.
        Romance about a band of Confederate soldiers who
     offer their services to Maximilian.

307 McClarren, James Kendall. Mexican Assignment. New
     York: Funk & Wagnalls, 1957.

308 McClung, Ahleen Masters. Mexican Mystique. México:
     Minutiae Mexicana, 1968.
        Short stories.

309 McClure, Michael. Ghost Tantras. San Francisco:
     City Lights, 1967.
        Includes some poems improvised in Mexico City.

310 McCulley, Johnston. A White Man's Chance. New
     York: G. H. Watt, 1927.
        Novel of adventure about the appearance of a mys-
     terious man in a sleepy village.

311   McDonald, Etta Austin Blaisdell, and Julia Dalrymple.
      Manuel in Mexico. Boston: Little, Brown, 1909.
      Children's story.

312   McLaughlin, Fred. The Blade of Picardy. Indianapolis:
      Bobbs-Merrill, 1928; London: Harper, 1929.
      Romance about a French swordsman in the court of
      Maximilian.

313   MacLeish, Archibald. Conquistador. Boston: Houghton
      Mifflin, 1932; London: V. Gollancz, 1933.
      Poem about the Conquest, as remembered by Bernal
      Díaz del Castillo. The American poet explored
      Cortés's route 1928-1929.

      McMorris, Helen and John. See Durfee, B.

314   McMurtry, Larry. The Last Picture Show. New York:
      Dial, 1966.
      Section of the novel concerns the adventures of two
      Texan youth in a border town.

315   McNally, E. Evalyn Grumbine. Patsy's Mexican Adven-
      ture. New York: Dodd, Mead, 1953.
      Novel for young readers. The author travelled in
      Mexico; see 906.

316   Madariaga y Rojo, Salvador de. El corazón de piedra
      verde. Buenos Aires: Sudamericano, 1943. The
      Heart of Jade. London: Collins, 1944; New York:
      Creative Age, 1944.
      Romance about the Conquest. The Spanish-born
      poet lived in Great Britain.

      Madden, Mabra. See Bryan, C.

317   Mailing, Arthur. Decoy. New York: Harper & Row, 1969.
      Novel of adventure about an American caught in
      financial intrigue in Mexico City.

318   Maitland, Edward. Higher Law. London: Chapman &
      Hall, 1870.

319   Malkus, Alida Sims. Caravans to Santa Fe. New York,
      London: Harper, 1928.
      Romance about the love between an American and
      a Spanish woman, set in New Mexico.

320 _____ . The Dark Star of Itza: The Story of a Pagan
    Princess. New York: Harcourt, Brace, 1930.
        Romance about a Maya princess at the time of the
        Toltec invasion.

321 _____ . A Fifth for the King: A Story of the Con-
    quest of Yucatan and of the Discovery of the Amazon.
    New York, London: Harper, 1931.
        Novel for young readers about the search of a
        Spanish boy for his brother.

322 _____ . The Spindle Imp, and Other Tales of Maya
    Myth and Folk Lore. New York: Harcourt, Brace,
    1931.
        Legends retold for children.

323 Mann, Edward Beverly. El Sombra. London: W. Col-
    lins, 1936; New York: W. Morrow, 1936.
        Western about two Americans.

324 Marryat, Frederick. Narrative of the Travels and Ad-
    ventures of Monsieur Violet in California, Sonora &
    Western Texas. Leipzig: B. Tauchnitz, 1843. The
    Travels and Romantic Adventures of Monsieur Violet
    among the Snake Indians and Wild Tribes of the Great
    Western Prairies. London: Longman, Brown, etc.,
    1843.
        Novel for young readers which plagiarized material
        from Josiah Gregg (782) and G. W. Kendall (847).

325 Marsh, Willard. Week with No Friday. New York:
    Harper & Row, 1965.
        Novel about American expatriates.

    Marshall, Arthur Calder. See Calder-Marshall, A.

326 Marshall, Edison. Cortez and Marina. Garden City:
    Doubleday, 1963.

327 Mason, Gregory. Green Gold of Yucatan. London:
    Hodder & Stoughton, 1926; New York: Duffield, 1926.
        Novel about two Americans in love with the same
        woman and their melodramatic adventures in Yuca-
        tán. The American journalist spent many years
        in Mexico; see 916-917.

328 _____ , and Richard Carroll. Mexican Gallop. New
    York: Green Circle, 1937.

Novel about a timid New Yorker who for a moment
joins the Mexican Revolution.

329 Maturin, Edward. Montezuma, the Last of the Aztecs.
New York: Paine & Burgess, 1845.

330 Maugham, William Somerset. Cosmopolitans: Very
Short Stories. London, Toronto: W. Heinemann,
1936. Cosmopolitans. Garden City: Doubleday,
Doran, 1936.
"The Bum" (short story): an English artist, down-
on-his-luck, in Veracruz. The English author
visited Mexico in 1924.

331 Mayer, Edwin L. No Man Alone. New York: Boni &
Gaer, 1948.
Novel of adventure about an American truckdriver
caught in financial intrigue.

332 Means, Florence Crannell. Adella Mary in Old New
Mexico. Boston: Houghton Mifflin, 1939.
Novel for teenagers about a girl's trip to Taos in
1846.

333 _____, and Carl Means. The Silver Fleece: A
Story of the Spanish in New Mexico. Philadelphia,
Toronto: J.C. Winston, 1950.
Novel for young readers about the return in 1695
of a Spanish family to New Mexico, from which
Indians had earlier driven them.

334 Mitchell, Ruth Comfort. Dust of Mexico. New York,
London: Appleton-Century, 1941.
Novel about an American librarian's journey to
Mexico, where three men become her suitors.

335 Moffett, Emma L. Crown Jewels, or The Dream of an
Empire. New York: Carleton, 1871. [From Wilgus]

336 Moon, Grace Purdie. Nadita (Little Nothing). Garden
City: Doubleday, Page, 1927; London: W. Heinemann, 1927.
Children's story about a Mexican girl's search for
a home.

337 _____. Solita. New York: Doubleday, Doran, 1938.
Children's story.

338 _____ . Tita of Mexico. New York: F. A. Stokes,
      1934.
         Novel for young readers about a Mexican girl in
         the Revolution.

339 Morris, Wright. The Field of Vision. New York:
      Harcourt, Brace, 1956; London: Weidenfeld & Nichol-
      son, 1957.
         Novel about the memories of several Americans
         watching a bullfight in Mexico City. The American
         author made three visits to Mexico, 1954 and 1958-
         1959.

340 _____ . Love among the Cannibals. New York:
      Harcourt, Brace, 1957; London: Weidenfeld & Nichol-
      son, 1958.
         Second half of the novel concerns the comic adven-
         tures of four Americans in Acapulco.

341 _____ . One Day. New York: Atheneum, 1965.
         Sections of the novel recall a Mexican's life in his
         old home and an American's visit in the 1930's.

342 Morrow, Elizabeth Cutter. The Painted Pig: A Mexi-
      can Picture Book. New York: Knopf, 1930.
         Children's story about two children's visit to a
         market. The American author was wife of the
         ambassador to Mexico; see 941-942.

343 Motley, Willard Francis. Let Noon Be Fair. London:
      Longmans, 1966; New York: Putnam, 1966.
         Unfinished novel about a Pacific fishing village and
         its invasion by expatriates. The American author
         lived in Mexico 1953-1965.

344 Mumsey, Nolie. Chac Mool, and Other Poems Relating
      to the Ruins of Yucatan. Denver: Range, 1958.

345 Munroe, Kirk. The White Conquerors: A Tale of
      Toltec and Aztec. New York: Scribner's, 1893; Lon-
      don: Blackie, 1894.

346 Murphy, Bill. The Red Sands of Santa Maria. New
      York: Dodd, Mead, 1956.
         Novel about a village bullfight.

347 Musick, John Roy. Humbled Pride: A Story of the
      Mexican War. New York: Funk & Wagnalls, 1893.

Neff, Priscilla Holton. See Holton, P.

348 Neiman, Gilbert. There Is a Tyrant in Every Country.
New York: Harcourt, Brace, 1947.
Novel of adventure about an American caught in
financial intrigue.

349 Nevins, Albert J. The Young Conquistador. New York:
Dodd, Mead, 1960.

350 Newcomb, Covelle. Silver Saddles. New York, Toron-
to: Longmans, Green, 1943.
Novel of adventure for young readers about an
American boy on a mission after a horse.

_____. Also see Burbank, A.

Nicholson, Helen. See Zglintzki, H. N.

Nicholson, Malcolm Wheeler. See Wheeler-Nicholson,
M.

351 Niggli, Josephina (also Josephine or Josefina). Mexi-
can Folk Plays, ed. Frederick Henry Koch. Chapel
Hill: University of North Carolina, 1938.
One-act plays; separate acting editions appeared of
"The Red Velvet Goat," "Soldadera," and "Sunday
Costs Five Pesos." The author was born in Monter-
rey of American parents and lived in Sabinas Hi-
dalgo 1920-1925.

352 _____. Mexican Silhouettes. San Antonio: Silhou-
ette, 1931.
Poems.

353 _____. Mexican Village. Chapel Hill: University
of North Carolina, 1945; London: S. Low, Marston,
1947.
Interrelated short stories about a Mexican-American who returns to his ancestors' village in northern Mexico.

354 _____. A Miracle for Mexico. Greenwich, Conn.:
New York Graphic Society, 1964.
Children's story about the Virgin of Guadalupe.

355 _____. Step Down, Elder Brother. New York:
Rinehart, 1947; London: S. Low, Marston, 1949.

Novel about an upper-class family in Monterrey and its problems of adjustment.

356 Nin, Anaïs. Collages. Chicago: Swallow, 1964; London: P. Owen, 1964.
Section of the novel takes place in Acapulco. The American author visited there 1947-1948.

357 _____. (a) Solar Barque. Ann Arbor: 1958. (b) Seduction of the Minotaur. Denver: Swallow, 1961; London: P. Owen, 1961.
Last of a novel series, set in a Pacific coast town modelled on Acapulco.

358 Noll, Arthur Howard, and Bourdon Wilson. In Quest of Aztec Treasure. New York: Neale, 1911.

359 Nordhoff, Walter (pseud. Antonio de Fierro Blanco). The Journey of the Flame; Being an Account of One Year in the Life of Señor Don Juan Obrigón, Known during Past Years in the Three Californias as Juan Colorado and to the Indiada of the Same as the Flame, Born at San José del Arroyo, Lower California, Mexico, in 1798, and, Having Seen Three Centuries Change Customs and Manners, Died Alone in 1902 at the Great Cardon near Rosario, Mexico, with His Face Turned to the South; Englished by Walter de Steiguer. Boston: Houghton Mifflin (Riverside), 1933.
Novel about a journey made by a Spanish boy from the tip of Baja California to San Francisco in 1810.

Norman, James. See Schmidt, J. N.

360 Nusser, J. L. The Burning Bridge. New York: Appleton-Century-Crofts, 1960.
Novel about an American expatriate in Guadalajara at a crisis in his life.

361 Ober, Frederick Albion. Montezuma's Gold Mines. Boston: D. Lothrop, 1888.
The author traveled in Mexico; see 953.

362 _____. The Silver City: A Story of Adventure in Mexico. Boston: D. Lothrop, 1883.

O'Connor, Patrick. See Wibberley, L. P. O.

363 O'Dell, Scott. The Black Pearl. Boston: Houghton
     Mifflin, 1967.
         Novel for young readers about a pearl fisher in
         Baja California.

364 _____. The King's Fifth. Boston: Houghton Mifflin,
     1966.
         Romance about Coronado's expedition.

365 _____. The Treasure of Topo-el-Bampo. Boston:
     Houghton Mifflin, 1972.

366 Olsen, Paul. The Virgin of San Gil. New York: Holt,
     Rinehart & Winston, 1965.
         Novel about an old Mexican peasant accused of steal-
         ing the statue of the Virgin from a church.

367 O'Rourke, Frank. The Far Mountains. New York:
     Morrow, 1959.
         Novel about the life of an Irish-American turned
         Spaniard in Taos between 1801 and 1848.

368 Osterhout, Hilda Marie. The Flame and the Serpent.
     New York: Dodd, Mead, 1948; London: V. Gollancz,
     1949.
         Novel about a young girl's visit.

369 Parish, Helen Rand. Our Lady of Guadalupe. New
     York: Viking, 1955.
         Legend of the Virgin of Guadalupe retold.

370 Parra, Rozelle S. On the Road to Anahuac: An Inci-
     dent in the Conquest of Mexico. New York: Vantage,
     1956.

371 Pease, Howard. Highroad to Adventure: What Happened
     to Tod Moran When He Travelled South into Old Mexi-
     co. New York: Doubleday, Doran, 1939.
         Mystery for teenagers.

372 Perkins, Charles Elliott. The Phantom Bull. Boston:
     Houghton Mifflin, 1932.

373 Perkins, Lucy Fitch. The Mexican Twins. Boston:
     Houghton Mifflin, 1915; London: J. Cape, 1955.
         Children's story.

374 Pike, Albert. (a) Prose Sketches and Poems Written
in the Western Country. Boston: Light & Horton,
1834. (b) Prose Sketches and Poems Written in the
Western Country, with Additional Stories, ed. David
J. Weber. Albuquerque: N. M. C. Horn, 1967.
(a-b) "A Mexican Tale" (short story), "War Song
of the Comanches," "Song of the Nabajo" (poems),
"The Inroad of the Nabajo," "Refugio" (short stories); (b) "A Journey to Xemes," "San Juan of the
Del Norte," "The Gachupin," "Manuel, the Wolf
Killer" (short stories). The first American fiction
and poetry based on actual experience in Mexico.
The author travelled in New Mexico 1831-1832.

375 Plagemann, Bentz. The Heart of Silence. New York:
Morrow, 1967.
Novel about an American's search for his brother,
who has disappeared into Mexico; with religious
themes.

376 Plummer, Mary Wright. Roy and Ray in Mexico. New
York: Holt, 1907.
Children's travel story.

377 Politi, Leo. Little Pancho. New York: Viking, 1938.

378 Porter, Katherine Anne. (a) Flowering Judas. New
York: Harcourt, Brace, 1930. (b) Hacienda. New
York: Harrison of Paris, 1934. (c) Flowering Judas,
and Other Stories. New York: Harcourt, Brace,
1935; London: J. Cape, 1936. (d) Collected Stories.
New York: Harcourt, Brace & World, 1965.
(a, c-d) "María Concepción," "Flowering Judas";
(b-d) "Hacienda"; (c-d) "That Tree"; (d) "Virgin
Violeta," "The Martyr" (short stories): lives of
Mexican Indians, aristocrats, and artists, an American teacher and a journalist, and Russian film-
makers. The American author lived in Mexico City
off and on 1920-1931; see 983.

379 _____. Ship of Fools. Boston: Little, Brown, 1962;
London: Secker & Warburg, 1962.
Opening scene of the novel occurs in Veracruz,
where various passengers, who have lived for some
time in different parts of the country, gather.

380 Porter, William Sydney (pseud. O. Henry). Options.

New York, London: Harper, 1909; London: Hodder &
Stoughton, 1916.
"He Also Serves" (short story): farce set in Maya
Yucatán. The American writer never visited Mexi-
co.

381 Potter, David. The Eleventh Hour. New York: Dodd,
Mead, 1910.

382 Purnell, Idella. Lost Princess of Yucatan. New York:
Holt, 1931.
Children's story about the friendship of an American
and an Indian girl. The American author lived in
Guadalajara during the 1920's.

383 _____. The Merry Frogs. Los Angeles: Suttonhouse, 1936.
Indian folk tales retold for children.

384 _____. Pedro, the Potter. New York: T. Nelson,
1935.
Children's story about a Mexican boy growing up in
a village of potters.

385 _____. The Wishing Owl: A Maya Storybook. New
York: Macmillan, 1931.
Folk tales retold for children.

386 _____, and John M. Weatherwax. The Talking Bird:
An Aztec Story Book; Tales Told to Little Paco by His
Grandfather. New York: Macmillan, 1930.
Folk tales retold for children.

387 Ramsey, Robert Waddy. Fiesta. New York: J. Day,
1955.
Novel about a Mexican peasant's escape to Mexico
City with an actress, who has come to make a
movie on his hacienda, and his return home.

388 Rathborne, St. George. The Young Range Riders, or
Two Yankee Cowboys on a Mexican Ranch. New York:
Street & Smith, 1902. The Young Range Riders.
London: S. Sibthorp, 1902.

389 Raymond, George Lansing (pseud. Walter Warren). The
Aztecs. Boston: Arena, 1894.
Play, later called The Aztec Gods.

390 Raynolds, Robert. Paquita. New York: G. P. Putnam's, 1947.
Historical novel about a Spanish girl.

Read, Georgia W. See Gaines, R. L.

391 Reed, John (Silas). Daughter of the Revolution, and Other Stories, ed. Floyd Dell. New York: Vanguard, 1927.
"Mac--American" and "Endymion, or On the Border" (short stories): Americans in the Mexican Revolution. The American author reported on Francisco Villa's campaign in 1913-1914; see 998.

Reid, Christian. See Tiernan, F.C.F.

392 Reid, (Thomas) Mayne. The Free Lances: A Romance of the Mexican Valley. London: Remington, 1881.

393 _____. The Lost Mountain: A Tale of Sonora. London: Routledge, 1885.

394 _____. The Queen of the Lakes: A Romance of the Mexican Valley. London: 1879.

395 _____. The Rifle Rangers, or Adventures of an Officer in Southern Mexico. London: 1850.

396 _____. The Scalp Hunters, or Romantic Adventures in Northern Mexico. London: 1851; Philadelphia: Lippincott, Grambo, 1851.

397 _____. The White Chief: A Legend of Northern Mexico. London: 1855; New York: G. W. Dillingham, 1891.
Novels [392-7] for teenagers. The British author was in Mexico during the Mexican-American War. See also 1149.

398 Reid, Thomasina Mary Eileen Boyd (pseud. Eileen Dwyer). The Kindly Gods. London: Hutchinson, 1933.

399 _____. Mexican Romance. London: Hutchinson, 1934.

400 Rembao, Alberto. Lupita: A Story of Mexico in Revolution. New York: Friendship, 1935.

Novel about three Mexicans in the Revolution. The
Mexican-born author was educated in the United
States.

401   Rexroth, Kenneth. The Collected Shorter Poems. New
        York: New Directions, 1966.
          "Oaxaca, 1925" and "Gradualism" (poems). The
          American poet visited Mexico City and Oaxaca in
          1925.

402   Rhoads, Dorothy. The Corn Grows Ripe. New York:
        Viking, 1956.
          Novel for young readers about a Maya boy.

403   Ripley, Clements. Dust and Sun. New York: Payson
        & Clarke, 1929; London: Hurst & Blackett, 1930.
          Novel of adventure involving an American.

404   Ritchie, Robert Welles. Drums of Doom. London:
        Hutchinson, 1923; New York: Dodd, Mead, 1923.
          Novel of adventure, set in Baja California, about
          the search for a stolen Murillo painting.

405   _____. Dust of the Desert. New York: Dodd,
        Mead, 1922; London: Hutchinson, 1923.
          Novel of adventure and romance between an Amer-
          ican and a Spanish woman, set along the border.

406   _____. Ho! Sonora. London: Hutchinson, 1925.

407   Roark, Garland. Star in the Rigging: A Novel of the
        Texas Navy. Garden City: Doubleday, 1954; London:
        Hodder & Stoughton, 1955.
          Novel of the Texas secession.

408   Rodney, George Brydges. Riders of the Chaparral.
        London: G.G. Harrap, 1935; New York: Greenberg,
        1935.
          Novel about a Mexican, at college in the United
          States, summoned back to participate in the Revolu-
          tion, and his involvement with an American girl.

      Roeburt, John. See Berle, M.

409   Ross, Patricia Fent. The Hungry Moon: Mexican
        Nursery Tales. New York: Knopf, 1946.
          Children's stories, based on Mexican nursery rhymes.

410 _____ . In Mexico They Say. New York: Knopf,
     1942.
          Folk tales retold for children.

411 Rotch, Francis. The Blue-Eyed God. Caldwell, Id.:
     Caxton, 1938.
          Historical romance for teenagers about a Toltec
          boy who befriends a shipwrecked Scandinavian,
          "Quetzalcóatl."

412 Rothermell, Fred. The Leaning Tower. London:
     T. Butterworth, 1934; New York: J. Day, 1934.
          Novel about a New York architect's fascination
          with Maya architecture and his visit to Yucatán.

413 Royle, Edwin Milton. Peace and Quiet. New York,
     London: Harper, 1916.
          Novel of adventure about an American in the Mexi-
          can Revolution.

414 Rukeyser, Muriel. Beast in View. Garden City:
     Doubleday, 1944.
          "Chapultepec Park I & II," "A Game of Ball,"
          "Gold Leaf," "All Souls," "Evening Plaza, San
          Miguel" (poems). The American poet made
          several visits to Mexico, beginning 1939.

415 _____ . The Green Wave. Garden City: Doubleday,
     1948.
          "A Charm for Cantinflas" (poem).

416 _____ . The Speed of Darkness. New York: Random
     House, 1968.
          "Cries from Chiapas" and "Silences of Volcanos"
          (poems).

417 _____ . Waterlily Fire: Poems, 1935-1962. New
     York: Macmillan, 1962.
          "For a Mexican Painter" (poem).

418 Rumaker, Michael. Gringoes, and Other Stories. New
     York: Grove, 1967.
          "Gringoes" (short story): Americans in a border
          town.

419 Runbeck, Margaret Lee. Pink Magic. Boston: Houghton
     Mifflin, 1949; London: P. Davies, 1951.

Novel for teenagers about an American girl's romantic adventures.

420 Ryan, Marah Ellis Martin. The Dancer of Tuluum. Chicago: A.C. McClurg, 1924.

421 _____. The Flute of the Gods. New York: F.A. Stokes, 1909.
Novel about the Pueblo Indians of the early 16th century.

422 _____. For the Soul of Rafael. Chicago: A.C. McClurg, 1906; London: C.F. Casenove, 1906.
Romance of the Spanish in California.

423 Salinas, Luis Omar. Crazy Gypsy. Fresno: La Raza Studies, 1970.
"Mexico Age Four" and "Mexico from a Taxi Cab" (poems).

424 Savage, Les. Doniphan's Ride. Garden City: Doubleday, 1959; London: Hamilton, 1963.
Novel about an American boy in the army during the Mexican-American War.

425 Sawyer, Ruth. The Least One. New York: Viking, 1941.
Children's story about a Mexican boy's faith in St. Francis to return his lost burro.

426 Schee, Oran Farelle (pseud. Kim Schee). Cantina. New York: Coward-McCann, 1941.
Short stories about Mexicans, recounted to an American sitting in a town cantina. The author lived in Mexico.

427 Schiller, Zoe Lund. Mexican Time. New York: Macmillan, 1943.
Novel about an American woman's romance with a Mexican ranch owner in Baja California.

428 Schloat, G. Warren Jr. Conchita and Juan: A Girl and Boy of Mexico. New York: Knopf, 1964.
Photographic story for young people.

429 Schmidt, James Norman (pseud. James Norman).

Juniper and the General. London: M. Joseph, 1956.
Father Juniper and the General. New York: Morrow,
1957.
    Novel about a new priest in a Mexican town. The
    author lived in Mexico.

430 Scoggins, Charles Elbert. The House of Darkness.
    Indianapolis: Bobbs-Merrill, 1931.
        Novel about a party which survives an airplane
        crash in Yucatán and finds a hidden Maya treasure
        house. The author lived in Mexico.

431 _____. The Proud Old Name. Indianapolis: Bobbs-
    Merrill, 1925.
        Novel about a comic romance.

432 Seifert, Shirley. The Turquoise Trail. Philadelphia:
    Lippincott, 1950; London: S. Paul, 1952.
        Novel based on the diary of Susan Shelby Magoffin
        (910), who travelled the Santa Fe trail at the time
        of the Mexican-American War.

433 Shaftel, George Armin. Golden Shore: A Novel of the
    Conquest of California. New York: Coward-McCann,
    1943.
        Novel about Americans in California in the 1840's.

434 Shellabarger, Samuel. Captain from Castile. Boston:
    Little, Brown, 1945; London: Macmillan, 1947.
        Romance of Spain and Mexico of the 16th century.

435 Silverberg, Robert. The Gate of Worlds. New York:
    Holt, Rinehart & Winston, 1967.
        Science fiction.

436 Simms, William Gilmore. The Vision of Cortes, Cain,
    and Other Poems. Charleston: J.S. Barges, 1829.
        "The Vision of Cortes" (epic poem).

437 Simon, Charlie May Hogue. Popo's Miracle. New
    York: E.P. Dutton, 1938.
        Children's story about a Mexican boy who is to
        become an artist.

438 Sitwell, Osbert. The Collected Satires and Poems.
    London: Duckworth, 1931.
        "Three Mexican Pieces" (poems).

439   Skinner, Constance Lindsay. The Ranch of the Golden
      Flowers. New York: Macmillan, 1928.

440   Small, Sidney Herschel. The Splendid Californians.
      Indianapolis: Bobbs-Merrill, 1928.
      Novel about the Spanish in California.

441   _____. Sword and Candle. Indianapolis: Bobbs-
      Merrill, 1927; London: Transworld, 1955.
      Novel about the Spanish conquest of California.

442   Smith, Arthur Douglas Howden. Conqueror: The Story
      of Cortes and Montezuma and the Slave Girl Malinal.
      Philadelphia: J.B. Lippincott, 1933.

      Smith, Joyce Collin. See Collin-Smith, J.

443   Smith, Susan Cowles. The Glories of Venus: A Novel
      of Modern Mexico. New York, London: Harper,
      1931.
      Novel of American and European expatriates in an
      art colony.

444   _____. Tranquilina's Paradise. New York: Minton,
      Balch, 1930.
      Fantasy for children about a woodcarver's objects,
      which come to life.

445   Smith, Wallace. The Little Tigress: Tales Out of the
      Dust of Mexico. New York, London: G.P. Putnam's,
      1923.
      Short stories.

446   Somerlott, Robert. The Flamingoes. Boston: Little,
      Brown, 1967.
      Novel about American expatriates in a coastal town.

447   _____. The Inquisitor's House. New York: Viking,
      1968; London: Hutchinson, 1969.

448   Sorensen, Virginia Eggerston. The Proper Gods. New
      York: Harcourt, Brace, 1951.
      Novel about a Yaqui Indian's return to his ancestral
      home after having lived in Arizona and having ex-
      perienced World War II.

449   Southern, Terry. Red-Dirt Marijuana, and Other Tastes.
      New York: New American Library, 1967.

"The Road Out of Axotle" (short story): night-
marish tale of an American driving.

450 Southey, Robert. Madoc. London: Longmans, 1805;
Boston: Munroe & Francis, 1806.
Epic poem about a Welsh prince and his encounter
with the Aztecs in their early days.

451 Spicer, Bart. The Day of the Dead. New York: Dodd,
Mead, 1955; London: Hodder & Stoughton, 1956.
Novel of Communist intrigue, centering around a
recently-arrived American.

452 Squier, Emma Lindsay. The Bride of the Sacred Well,
and Other Tales of Ancient Mexico. New York:
Cosmopolitan Book, 1928.
The American author travelled in Mexico; see 1057.

453 Stacton, David Derek. A Signal Victory. London:
Faber & Faber, 1960; New York: Pantheon, 1962.
Novel about Guerrero, Spanish sailor shipwrecked
off the coast of Yucatán in 1511, and his subsequent life with the Mayas.

454 Steell, Willis. Isidra. Boston: Ticknor, 1883; London: F. T. Neely, 1897.

455 Steinbeck, John. The Forgotten Village.... New York:
Viking, 1941.
Fictional form of the film script. The American
writer went on location in 1940.

456 _____ . The Pearl. New York: Viking, 1947; London: W. Heinemann, 1948.
Novel about the evil which befalls a La Paz pearl
fisher and his family when he finds a large pearl.
The author sailed the Gulf of California in 1940;
see 1065.

457 Stevens, Wallace. Harmonium. 2nd ed. New York:
Knopf, 1931.
"The Comedian as the Letter C," "Sea Surface
Full of Clouds," and "The Revolutionists Stop for
Orangeade" (poems). The American author did
not visit Mexico.

458 Stoker, Catherine Ulmer. Little Daughter of Mexico.

Dallas: Dealey & Lowe, 1937.
The author travelled in Mexico; see 1071.

459   Storm, Dan. Picture Tales from Mexico. New York:
F.A. Stokes, 1941.
Animal folk tales retold for children.

460   Storm, Marian. Poems of Sun and Snow. México:
American Book Store, 1955.

461   _____. True Stories from Tarascan Places. México: 1941.
The author lived in Mexico; see 1076-1077.

462   Strabel, Thelma. Storm to the South. Garden City:
Doubleday, Doran, 1944; London: Collins, 1945.
Romance of adventure in Peru and California.

463   Stratemeyer, Edward (pseud. Capt. Ralph Bonehill).
For the Liberty of Texas. Boston: D. Estes, 1900.
Novel for teenagers about the Texas secession.

464   _____. Under Scott in Mexico. Boston: D. Estes,
1902.

465   _____. With Taylor on the Rio Grande. Boston:
D. Estes, 1901.
Novels [464-465] for teenagers about the Mexican-
American War.

466   Summers, Hollis Spurgeon. The Weather of February.
New York: Harper, 1957.
Novel about a crippled American woman, remember-
ing in Mexico City her past life.

467   Summers, Richard Aldrich. Cavalcade to California.
London: Oxford University, 1941.
Novel for teenagers about the Spanish settlement
of San Francisco.

468   _____. The Devil's Highway. New York: T. Nelson, 1937.
Romance for teenagers about the Spanish exploration of northern Mexico and Baja California.

469   Swarthout, Glendon Fred. They Came to Cordura.
London: Heinemann, 1958; New York: Random House,
1958.

Novel concerned with John Pershing's 1916 expedition against Francisco Villa.

470   Tallman, Robert. Adios, O'Shaughnessy. Garden City: Doubleday, 1950.
Novel about Americans in a remote town.

471   Tanner, Edward Everett (pseud. Patrick Dennis). Genius. New York: Harcourt, Brace, 1962; London: A. Barker, 1963.
Novel about a movie director come to Mexico City and the film he makes.

472   Tarshis, Elizabeth Kent. The Village That Learned to Read. Boston: Houghton Mifflin, 1941.
Children's story about a Mexican boy who wanted to be a bullfighter and thus saw no reason to learn to read.

473   Taylor, Grant. Gunsmoke Hacienda. Philadelphia: J. B. Lippincott, 1936; London: Skeffington, 1937.
Western.

474   Taylor, Robert Lewis. Two Roads to Guadalupé. Garden City: Doubleday, 1964; London: A. Deutsch, 1965.
Picaresque novel about two boys in the Mexican-American War. The American author travelled in Mexico.

475   Teilhet, Darwin Le Ora. The Road to Glory. New York: Funk & Wagnalls, 1956.
Novel about Father Junípero Serra in California in 1783.

476   Thomas, Margaret Loring. The Burro's Moneybag. New York: Abingdon, 1931.
Children's story about a Mexican boy who wants to buy his own burro.

477   _____. Carlos, Our Mexican Neighbor. Indianapolis: Bobbs-Merrill, 1938.
Children's story about a Mexican boy and how he helps build his village school.

478   Thompson, Edward Herbert. Children of the Cave. Boston: Marshall Jones, 1929.

Novel about three children, born in Yucatán of American parents, wandering through a cave in which they had sought to escape a revolution. The American author worked in Mexico; see 1090.

479 Thorpe, Francis Newton. The Spoils of Empire: A Romance of the Old World and the New. Boston: Little, Brown, 1903.

480 Tiernan, Frances Christine Fisher (pseud. Christian Reid). The Land of the Sun: Vistas Mexicanas. New York: D. Appleton, 1894.

481 _____. The Picture of Las Cruces: A Romance of Mexico. New York: D. Appleton, 1896.
The American author lived in Mexico 1888-1898.

482 Toepperwein, Fritz Arnold. José and the Mexican Jumping Bean. Boerne, Tex.: Highland, 1965.

483 Tonna, Charlotte Elizabeth Browne (pseud. Charlotte Elizabeth). Izram: A Mexican Tale; and Other Poems. London: J. Nisbet, 1826. The Convent Bell, and Other Poems. New York: J.S. Taylor, 1845.
"Izram: A Mexican Tale" (epic poem).

484 Traven, B. (Traven Torsvan). Die Baumwollpflücker. Berlin: Buchmeister-Verlag, 1929. The Cotton Pickers, trans. Eleanor Brockett. London: R. Hale, 1956. The Cotton-Pickers. New York: Hill & Wang, 1969.
Picaresque novel about an American working at various jobs in northeastern Mexico. The American-born author lived in Mexico from the early 1920's until his death. See also 1099.

485 _____. Die Brücke im Dschungel. Berlin: Büchergilde Gutenberg, 1929. The Bridge in the Jungle. New York: Knopf, 1938; London: J. Cape, 1940.
Novel about a child's death and funeral in southern Mexico.

486 _____. (a) Der Busch. Berlin: Büchergilde Gutenberg, 1928. (b) Canasta de cuentos mexicanos, trans. Rosa Elena Luján. México: 1956. (c) Stories by

the Man Nobody Knows: Nine Tales. Evanston, Ill.:
Regency, 1961. (d) The Night Visitor, and Other
Stories. New York: Hill & Wang, 1966; London:
Cassell, 1967.
    Short stories about Mexicans and some Americans.

487   . Ein General kommt aus dem Dschungel.
Amsterdam: A. de Lange, 1940. General from the
Jungle, trans. Desmond I. Vessey. London: R.
Hale, 1954.
    Sixth novel of the Jungle Series, about the after-
math of a successful uprising by Indians in southern
Mexico against the plantations, coinciding with the
Mexican Revolution.

488   . Der Karren. Berlin: Büchergilde Gutenberg, 1930. The Carreta, trans. Basil Creighton.
London: Chatto & Windus, 1935. The Carreta. New
York: Hill & Wang, 1970.
    First novel of the Jungle Series, about an ox-cart
driver and how he joins the workers for a mahogany
plantation.

489   . Macario, trans. Hans Kandus. Zürich:
Büchergilde Gutenberg, 1950.
    Short story about a woodchopper's fantasy, set dur-
ing the time of Spanish rule. Printed in English
in 486 (d).

490   . Der Marsch ins Reich des Caoba: Ein
Kriegsmarsch. Zürich: Büchergilde Gutenberg, 1933.
March to Caobaland. London: R. Hale, 1961. March
to the Monteria. New York: Dell, 1964.
    Third novel of the Jungle Series, about the march
of the workers to the mahogany plantation.

491   . Die Rebellion der Gehenkten. Zürich:
Büchergilde Gutenberg, 1936. The Rebellion of the
Hanged, trans. Charles Duff. London: R. Hale,
1952. The Rebellion of the Hanged, trans. from
Spanish. New York: Knopf, 1952.
    Fifth novel of the Jungle Series, about the Indians'
uprising against the mahogany plantation.

492   . Regierung. Berlin: Büchergilde Gutenberg,
1931. Government, trans. Basil Creighton. London:

Chatto & Windus, 1935. Government. New York: Hill & Wang, 1971.
Second novel of the Jungle Series, about Mexican politics and the internal government of an Indian village and how some villagers are sold as workers to a mahogany plantation.

493   . Der Schatz der Sierra Madre. Berlin: Büchergilde Gutenberg, 1927. The Treasure of the Sierra Madre, trans. Basil Creighton. London: Chatto & Windus, 1934. The Treasure of the Sierra Madre. New York: Knopf, 1935.
Novel about three American gold prospectors.

494   . Sonnen-Schöpfung: Indianische Legende. Zürich: Büchergilde Gutenberg, 1936. The Creation of the Sun and the Moon. New York: Hill & Wang, 1968.
Indian legends.

495   . Die Troza. Zürich: Büchergilde Gutenberg, 1936.
Fourth novel of the Jungle Series, about life on the mahogany plantation.

496   . Die Weisse Rose. Berlin: Büchergilde Gutenberg, 1929. The White Rose. London: R. Hale, 1965.
Novel about the machinations of an American oil company against an Indian hacienda.

497 Treadwell, Sophie. Lusita. New York: Cape & Smith, 1931.
Novel about an American journalist who discovers that a Mexican woman, kidnapped by an outlaw, had sought him out in order to escape her upperclass home.

498 Treviño, Elizabeth Borton. Even as You Love. New York: Crowell, 1957.
Novel about an American woman, separated from her husband, who comes to Mexico City to live with her sister and Mexican brother-in-law. The American author married a Mexican and lived in Monterrey, Mexico City, and Cuernavaca; see 1102-1103.

499 _____ . The Fourth Gift. Garden City: Doubleday,
        1966.
        Novel about the church war in Jalisco in the 1920's.

500 _____ . The House on Bitterness Street. Garden
        City: Doubleday, 1970.
        Novel about a woman attached to the home in Mexi-
        co City where she had been born and her attempt
        to possess and keep it.

501 _____ . Nacar, the White Deer. New York: Farrar,
        Straus, 1963; Kingswood, Eng.: Worlds Work, 1964.
        Children's story.

502 _____ (as Elizabeth Borton). Our Little Aztec Cous-
        in of Long Ago; Being the Story of Coyotl and How He
        Won Honor under His King. Boston: L.C. Page,
        1934.
        Children's story.

503 _____ . Pollyanna's Castle in Mexico. Boston:
        L.C. Page, 1934; London: G.G. Harrap, 1935.
        Novel for young readers.

504 Treynor, Albert M. Hands Up! New York: Dodd,
        Mead, 1928.
        Novel about an American caught in intrigue.

505 Venable, Clarke. All the Brave Rifles. Chicago:
        Reilly & Lee, 1929.
        Novel about the Texas secession.

506 Vidal, Gore. The City and the Pillar. New York:
        Dutton, 1948; London: J. Lehmann, 1949.
        Middle section of the novel takes its American
        homosexual hero to Mérida with friends.

507 Wadleigh, John. Bitter Passion. London: P. Davies,
        1959; New York: Dutton, 1959.
        Novel about the conflicts between American ex-
        patriates and the natives.

508 Wagner, Blanche Collet. Tales of Mayaland. Pasadena:
        San Pasqual, 1938.
        Historical short stories for children.

509   Wagner, Geoffrey Atheling.   The Passionate Land.
      New York: Simon & Schuster, 1953; London: Ward,
      Lock, 1956.
            Novel of murder and intrigue, involving British,
            American, and Mexican characters.

510   Walker, Cora.   Cuatemo, Last of the Aztec Emperors.
      New York: Dayton, 1934.

511   Wallace, Irving Speed.   Mystery in the Tropics.   Chi-
      cago: A. Whitman, 1941.

512   Wallace, Lewis.   The Fair God, or The Last of the
      'Tzins: A Tale of the Conquest of Mexico.   Boston:
      J. R. Osgood, 1873; London: F. Warne, 1887.
            Romance of the Conquest.   The American author
            was in Mexico during the Mexican-American War
            and later worked against Maximilian.   See 1118.

      Warren, Walter.   See Raymond, G. L.

513   Waters, Frank.   The Dust within the Rock.   New York:
      Liveright, 1940.
            The American author made several expeditions into
            remote areas of Mexico, beginning in the late
            1920's; see 1124.

514   _____.   Fever Pitch.   New York: Liveright, 1930.
            Novel about a Mexican girl and an American engi-
            neer lured to the desert in search of gold.

      Weatherwax, John M.   See Purnell, I.

515   Weil, Ann.   The Silver Faun.   Indianapolis: Bobbs-
      Merrill, 1939.
            Children's story about a Mexican boy who works
            for a Taxco art shop (i. e. for William Spratling).

      Weil, Truda T.   See Kohan, F. H.

516   Wellman, Paul Iselin.   Angel with Spurs.   Philadelphia:
      J. B. Lippincott, 1942; London: Cassell, 1948.
            Romance about the band of Confederate soldiers
            who wanted to join Maximilian.

517   _____.   The Iron Mistress.   Garden City: Double-
      day, 1951; London: W. Laurie, 1952.

Novel about James Bowie, including his role in the Texas secession.

518 Wheeler-Nicholson, Malcolm. The Corral of Death.
     Boston: Houghton Mifflin, 1929.
     Novel of adventure set along the border during the
     Mexican Revolution.

519 Whitaker, Herman. The Mystery of the Barranca.
     New York, London: Harper, 1913.
     Novel about two American engineers operating a
     copper mine.

520 _____. Over the Border. New York, London:
     Harper, 1917; London: W. Collins, 1924.

521 _____. The Planter. New York, London: Harper,
     1909; London: W. Collins, 1921.
     Novel about the harsh life of the workers on a
     Mexican rubber plantation.

522 White, Steward Edward. Folded Hills. Garden City:
     Doubleday, Doran, 1934; London: Hodder & Stoughton,
     1934.

523 _____. The Long Rifle. Garden City: Doubleday,
     Doran, 1932; London: Hodder & Stoughton, 1932.

524 _____. Ranchero. Garden City: Doubleday, Doran,
     1933; London: Hodder & Stoughton, 1933.
     Trilogy [522-4] about a mountain man who moves
     to California and acquires a Spanish wife; time is
     the 1820's until the Mexican-American War.

525 Wibberley, Leonard Patrick O'Connor. The Island of
     the Angels. New York: W. Morrow, 1965.
     Novel of adventure about a hermit fisherman's
     encounter with an orphan boy and his attempt to
     help him during a raging storm. The author
     travelled in Baja California.

526 _____ (pseud. Patrick O'Connor). Mexican Road
     Race. New York: Washburn, 1957.
     Novel for teenagers about the American winner of
     the car race. See 1138.

527 Wilder, Robert. Fruit of the Poppy. London: W. H. Allen,
     1965; New York: Putnam, 1965.

528   Willard, Theodore Arthur.   Bride of the Rain God:
      Princess of Chichen-Itza, the Sacred City of the
      Mayas; Being an Historical Romance of a Prince and
      a Princess of Chichen-Itza in That Glamorous Land
      of the Ancient Mayas, Where Conflicting Human Pas-
      sions Dominated the Lives of the Long-Dead Past as
      They Do Those of Today.   Cleveland: Burrows, 1930.
      The American author lived in Yucatán; see 1141.

529   _____.   The Wizard of Zacna, Lost City of the
      Mayas: Remarkable Adventures of an Ahmen, Wizard
      and Mystic of Yucatan, in an Unknown Country to
      Which the Ancient Mayas Had Fled, Leaving Their
      Great Stone Cities Silent and Desolate to Be Overgrown
      with Forest and Jungle.   Boston: Stratford, 1929.
      Novel showing the parallels between the love stories
      of a dying Maya and an American explorer.

530   Willets, Gilson.   The Double Cross: A Romance of
      Mystery and Adventure in Mexico of To-Day.   London:
      T. F. Unwin, 1910; New York: G. W. Dillingham,
      1910.
      Mystery involving an American and two Spanish
      women.

531   Williams, Dorothy Jeanne (pseud. J. R. Williams).   Mis-
      sion in Mexico.   Englewood Cliffs, N. J.:   Prentice-
      Hall, 1959.
      Novel for young readers about an American boy in
      search of his father, an ex-Confederate who had
      joined Maximilian.

532   Williams, Tennessee (Thomas Lanier).   (a) American
      Blues.   New York: Dramatists Play Service, 1948.
      (b) Camino Real.   New York: New Directions, 1953;
      London: Secker & Warburg, 1958.
      The shorter version included in (a), "Ten Blocks
      on the Camino Real," has more Mexican elements
      than the full-length play, a fantasy about trapped
      people seeking a way out.

533   _____.   In the Winter of Cities.   New York: New
      Directions, 1956.
      "The Christus of Guadalajara" (poem).

534   _____.   The Night of the Iguana.   New York: New
      Directions, 1962; London: Secker & Warburg, 1963.

Play about several Americans who end up at a
hotel near Acapulco in 1940. The American play-
wright lived in Acapulco and Chapala in the 1940's.

535 _____. One Arm, and Other Stories. New York:
New Directions, 1948. Three Players of a Summer
Game, and Other Stories. London: Secker & Warburg, 1960.
"The Night of the Iguana" (short story): an American woman's experience with two homosexuals in
a hotel near Acapulco.

536 Williams, William Carlos. The Desert Music, and
Other Poems. New York: Random House, 1954. Pictures from Brueghel. London: MacGibbon & Kee, 1963.
"The Desert Music" (poem): personal observations
based on a visit to Juárez in 1950.

537 Williamson, Thames Ross. Sad Indian: A Novel about
Mexico. New York: Harcourt, Brace, 1932; London:
J. Cape, 1933.
Novel about the problems which befall an Indian
who comes to Mexico City.

Wilson, Bourdon. See Noll, A. H.

538 Wilson, Carter. Crazy February. Philadelphia: Lippincott, 1966.
Novel about the Maya Indians of southern Mexico.

Wilson, Charlotte. See Baker, K. W.

539 Wilson, Eleanor Hubbard. The Magical Jumping Beans.
New York: E. P. Dutton, 1939.
Children's story about a Mexican boy who leaps
through his country's history as a result of the
magic beans.

540 Wolfe, Bernard. The Great Prince Died. London: J.
Cape, 1959; New York: Scribner, 1959.
Novel based upon the death of Leon Trotsky.

541 Woodard, Stacy, and Horace Woodard. The Adventures
of Chico, a Small Mexican Boy Who Has Many Animal
Friends. New York: Stackpole, 1938.
Children's story.

542 Woods, Clee. <u>Riders of the Sierra Madre.</u> New York:
     Macaulay, 1935.
     Western.

543 Wormser, Richard Edward. <u>Battalion of Saints.</u> New
     York: D. McKay, 1961.
     Novel about Mormons in the Mexican-American
     War.

544 Zglintzki, Helen Nicholson de (Helen Nicholson). <u>The
     Purple Silences.</u> London: S. Low, Marston, 1924.

545 Ziegler, Isabelle Gibson. <u>The Nine Days of Father
     Serra.</u> New York: Longmans, Green, 1951.
     Novel about Father Junípero Serra in California
     in 1769.

546 Zieman, Irving Pergament. <u>Mexican Mosaic.</u> Boston:
     Forum, 1964.
     Poems.

A CHECKLIST OF AMERICAN AND BRITISH TRAVEL
BOOKS, MEMOIRS, AND OTHER PERSONAL
OBSERVATIONS ABOUT MEXICO (1569-1972)

547 Adams, Agatha Boyd. A Journey to Mexico. Chapel
Hill: University of North Carolina, 1945.

548 Adams, Henry (Brooks). Henry Adams and His Friends:
A Collection of His Unpublished Letters, ed. Harold
Dean Cater. Boston: Houghton Mifflin, 1947.

549 _____. Letters, 1892-1918, ed. Worthington Chauncey
Ford. Boston: Houghton Mifflin, 1938.
The American author made two visits to Mexico
City, 1894-1895 and 1896, meeting the president
on the last.

550 Adventures in Search of a Living in Spanish-America;
by "Vaquero." London: J. Bale, 1911.

551 Aiken, Conrad Potter. Ushant: An Essay. New York:
Duell, Sloan & Pearce, 1952.
Fictionalized autobiography, including comments
about the American poet's 1937 visit to Malcolm
Lowry in Cuernavaca to obtain a divorce and the
writing of his Mexican novel (see 1).

552 Aldrich, Lorenzo D. A Journal of the Overland Route
to California & the Gold Mines. Lansingburgh, N.Y.:
1851.

553 Allen, G.N. Mexican Treacheries and Cruelties: Incidents and Sufferings in the Mexican War, with Accounts of Hardships Endured, Treacheries of the Mexicans, Battles Fought and Success of American Arms
.... Boston: 1847.

554 Allen, Lewis Leonidas. Pencillings of Scenes upon the
Rio Grande; Originally Pub. bu [sic] the Saint Louis
American. 2nd ed. New York: 1848.

64

555 Anderson, Robert. An Artillery Officer in the Mexican
    War, 1846-7: Letters of Robert Anderson, Captain
    3rd Artillery, U.S.A., ed. Eba Anderson Lawton.
    New York, London: Putnam's, 1911.

556 Anderson, Sherwood. Sherwood Anderson's Memoirs:
    A Critical Edition, ed. Ray Lewis White. Chapel
    Hill: University of North Carolina, 1969.
        "Mexican Night" (essay): an episode from the
    American writer's 1938 visit, quite different from
    the short story originally published (see 6).

557 Anderson, William Marshall. An American in Maxi-
    milian's Mexico, 1865-1866: The Diaries of William
    Marshall Anderson, ed. Ramón Eduardo Ruiz. San
    Marino, Calif.: Huntington Library, 1959.

    Anson, George. See Walter, R.

558 Arthur, Jan, and Barb Coleman. Aztec Trek. Denver:
    A&C, 1965.

559 Aubertin, John James. A Flight to Mexico. London:
    K. Paul, 1882.

560 Audubon, John Woodhouse. Audubon's Western Journal,
    1849-1850; Being the Ms. Record of a Trip from New
    York to Texas and an Overland Journey through Mexi-
    co and Arizona to the Gold Fields of California, ed.
    Frank Heywood Hodder. Cleveland: A.H. Clark,
    1906.

561 _____. Illustrated Notes of an Expedition through
    Mexico and California. New York: J.W. Audubon,
    1852.

562 Augur, Helen. Zapotec. Garden City: Doubleday,
    1954.

563 Austin, Mary Ann Van Ness. Byways to Mexico.
    New York: Savoy, 1940.

564 Austin, Mary Hunter. Earth Horizon. Boston:
    Houghton Mifflin, 1932.
        Autobiography, including a brief account of the
    American writer's visit with Diego Rivera in
    Mexico City.

565 Austin, Moses, and Stephen Fuller Austin. The Austin
     Papers, ed. Eugene Campbell Barker. Washington:
     Government Printing Office, 1924-1928 (v. 1-2);
     Austin: University of Texas, 1927 (v. 3).
         Letters and documents from two leaders of the
         American settlement of Texas.

566 Baerlein, Henry Philip Bernard. The Caravan Rolls
     On. London: F. Muller, 1944.
         "Mexico": the English author lived there for some
         years. See also 12.

567 Bailey, Helen Miller. Santa Cruz of the Etla Hills.
     Gainesville: University of Florida, 1958.

568 Baker, Frank Collins. A Naturalist in Mexico; Being
     a Visit to Cuba, Northern Yucatan, and Mexico.
     Chicago: Oliphant, 1895.

569 Baldridge, Michael. A Reminiscence of the Parker H.
     French Expedition through Texas & Mexico to Cali-
     fornia in the Spring of 1850, ed. John B. Goodman
     III. Los Angeles: 1959.

570 Ballentine, George. Autobiography of an English Soldier
     in the United States Army. London: Hurst & Blackett,
     1853.
         Memoirs, including experiences in the Mexican-
         American War.

571 Ballou, Maturin Murray. Aztec Land. Boston:
     Houghton Mifflin, 1890.

572 Bancroft, Hubert Howe. Literary Industries: A Mem-
     oir. New York: Harper, 1891.
         Memoirs, including accounts of the American his-
         torian's two visits to Mexico City and meeting with
         the president.

573 Bandelier, Adolph Francis Alphonse. A Scientist on the
     Trail: Travel Letters..., 1880-1881, ed. George
     Peter Hammond and Edgar F. Goad. Berkeley:
     Quivira Society, 1949.
         Letters written in German (here translated) for an
         American newspaper by the Swiss-American ar-
         chaeologist.

574 Banning, George Hugh. In Mexican Waters. Boston:
     C.E. Lauriat, 1925; London: M. Hopkinson, 1925.
     Account of a cruise along the Pacific coast.

575 Barber, Amherst Willoughby, ed. The Benevolent Raid
     of General Lew Wallace: How Mexico Was Saved in
     1864; The Monroe Doctrine in Action; Testimony of
     a Survivor, Private Justus Brooks. Washington:
     Beresford, 1914.

576 Barbour, Philip Norbourne, and Martha Isabella Hopkins
     Barbour. Journals of the Late Brevet Major Philip
     Norbourne Barbour and His Wife..., Written during
     the War with Mexico--1846, ed. Rhoda van Bibber
     Tanner Doubleday. New York: Putnam's, 1936.

577 Barretto, Laurence Brevoort (Larry). Bright Mexico.
     New York: Farrar & Rinehart, 1935.
     Account of a visit made by the author and his wife.

578 Bartlett, John Russell. Personal Narrative of Explora-
     tions and Incidents in Texas, New Mexico, California,
     Sonora, and Chihuahua, Connected with the United
     States and Mexican Boundary Commission during the
     Years '51, '52, and '53. London: Routledge, 1854;
     New York: Appleton, 1854.

579 Barton, Mary. Impressions of Mexico with Brush and
     Pen. London: Methuen, 1911.

     Barton, Rex. See Thomas, L.J.

580 Bates, James Hale. Notes of a Tour in Mexico and
     California. New York: Burr, 1887.

581 Baxter, Sylvester. The Cruise of a Land Yacht.
     Boston: Authors' Mutual, 1891.

582 Beals, Carleton. Brimstone and Chili: A Book of
     Personal Experiences in the Southwest and in Mexico.
     New York: Knopf, 1927.

583   . Glass Houses: Ten Years of Free-Lancing.
     Philadelphia: Lippincott, 1938.

584   . The Great Circle: Further Adventures in
     Free-Lancing. Philadelphia: Lippincott, 1940.

585   . House in Mexico. New York: Hastings
     House, 1958.
          Four memoirs [582-585], each concerned in large
          part or altogether with the American journalist's
          life in Mexico City during the 1920's and part of
          the 1930's.

586   . Mexican Maze. Philadelphia, London: Lip-
     pincott, 1931.
          Interpretation of present-day conditions, based upon
          the author's personal observations. See also 33-35.

587 Bean, Ellis P. Memoir of Col. Ellis P. Bean, Written
     by Himself about the Year 1816, ed. W. P. Yoakum.
     Houston: Book Club of Texas, 1930.
          First printed in History of Texas from the First
          Settlement in 1685 to Its Annexation by the United
          States in 1846, by Henderson K. Yoakum (New
          York: Redfield, 1856). Memoir of an early Texas
          settler.

588 Bean, Lowell John, and William Mervin Mason, eds.
     Diaries & Accounts of the Romero Expeditions in
     Arizona and California, 1823-1826. Palm Springs,
     Calif.: Palm Springs Desert Museum, 1962.

589 Beaufoy, Mark. Mexican Illustrations, Founded upon
     Facts, Indicative of the Present Condition of Society,
     Manners, Religion, and Morals among the Spanish and
     Native Inhabitants of Mexico, with Observations upon
     the Government and Resources of the Republic of
     Mexico as They Appeared during Part of the Years
     1825, 1826, and 1827.... London: Carpenter, 1828.

590 Becher, Henry C. R. A Trip to Mexico; Being Notes
     of a Journey from Lake Erie to Lake Tezcuco and
     Back... Toronto: Willing & Williamson, 1880.

591 Beckwourth, James P. (as told to T. D. Bonner). The
     Life and Adventures of James P. Beckwourth, Moun-
     taineer, Scout, and Pioneer, and Chief of the Crow
     Nation of Indians. New York: Harper, 1856; London:
     Unwin, 1892.

592 Bedford, Sybille. The Sudden View: A Mexican Jour-
     ney. London: V. Gollancz, 1953; New York: Harper,
     1953.
          Account of a visit made by the English author.

593 Beebe, Charles William. Book of Bays. New York:
     Harcourt, Brace, 1942; London: Bodley Head, 1947.
     Account of an expedition made by the naturalist
     along the Pacific coast.

594   . Two Bird-Lovers in Mexico. Boston:
     Houghton Mifflin, 1905; London: Constable, 1905.
     Account of a winter spent in the interior by the
     author and his wife.

595   . Zaca Venture. London: J. Lane, 1938; New
     York: Harcourt, Brace, 1938.
     Account of a 1936 expedition in the Gulf of Califor-
     nia.

596 Beechey, Frederick William. Narrative of a Voyage to
     the Pacific and Beering's Strait to Co-operate with the
     Polar Expeditions, Performed in His Majesty's Ship
     Blossom under Command of Captain F.W. Beechey in
     the Years 1825, 26, 27, 28. London: H. Colburn &
     R. Bentley, 1831; Philadelphia: Corey & Lea, 1832.

597 Bell, Horace. On the Old West Coast; Being Further
     Reminiscences of a Ranger, ed. Lanier Bartlett.
     New York: Grosset & Dunlap, 1930.

598   . Reminiscences of a Ranger, or Early Times
     in Southern California. Los Angeles: Yarnell,
     Gaystile & Mathes, 1881.

599 Benham, Henry Washington. Recollections of Mexico
     and the Battle of Buena Vista, Feb. 22 and 23, 1847.
     Boston: 1871.

600 Betagh, William. A Voyage Round the World; Being an
     Account of a Remarkable Enterprize Begun in 1719,
     Chiefly to Cruise on the Spaniards in the Great South
     Ocean.... London: T. Combes, 1728.

601 Bieber, Ralph Paul, ed. Marching with the Army of
     the West, 1846-1848; by Abraham Robinson Johnston,
     Marcellus Ball Edwards, and Philip Gooch Ferguson.
     Glendale, Calif.: A.H. Clark, 1936.

602   , ed. Southern Trails to California in 1849.
     Glendale, Calif.: A.H. Clark, 1937.

603 Bigler, Henry William. Bigler's Chronicle of the West:
     The Conquest of California, Discovery of Gold, and
     Mormon Settlement as Reflected in Henry William
     Bigler's Diaries, ed. Erwin Gustav Gudde. Berkeley:
     University of California, 1962.

604 Billings, Eliza Allen. The Female Volunteer, or The
     Life and Wonderful Adventures of Miss Eliza Allen,
     a Young Lady of Eastport, Maine. N.p.: 1851.
     Memoir, including experiences in the Mexican-
     American War.

605 Billings, Frederick. Letters from Mexico, 1859, ed.
     Mary M. Billings French. Woodstock, Vt.: 1936.
     [From Gardiner]

606 Bishop, William Henry. Old Mexico and Her Lost
     Provinces: A Journey in Mexico, Southern California,
     and Arizona, by Way of Cuba. London: Chatto &
     Windus, 1883; New York: Harper, 1883.
     See also 47.

607 Blake, Mary Elizabeth, and Margaret Frances Buchanan
     Sullivan. Mexico: Picturesque, Political, Progres-
     sive. Boston: Lee & Shephard, 1888.

608 Blichfeldt, Emil Harry. A Mexican Journey. New
     York: Crowell, 1912.
     Impressions of Veracruz, Mexico City, and
     Tehauntepec.

     Bodenham, Roger. See Hakluyt, R.

609 Bowles, Paul. Without Stopping: An Autobiography.
     Boston: Putnam, 1972.
     Memoirs, including account of the years spent by
     the American author and his wife, Jane Bowles, in
     Acapulco in the early 1940's.

610 Bowman, Heath, and Stirling Dickinson. Mexican
     Odyssey. Chicago: Willett, Clark, 1935.
     Account of a six-months visit made by the Amer-
     ican writer and the American painter. See also
     54.

611 Box, Michael James. Capt. James Box's Adventures
     and Explorations in New and Old Mexico; Being the

Record of Ten Years of Travel and Research...
New York: J. Miller, 1869.

612   Brackenridge, Henry Marie.   Mexican Letters Written
      during the Progress of the Late War between the
      United States and Mexico.   Washington: R.A. Waters,
      1850.

613   Brackett, Albert Gallatin.   General Lane's Brigade in
      Central Mexico.   Cincinnati: H.W. Derby, 1854.

614   Braddy, Haldeen.   Mexico and the Old Southwest:
      People, Palaver, Places.   Port Washington, N.Y.:
      Kennikat, 1971.
      Articles about life on the border (El Paso area).

615   Brand, Donald Dilworth.   Mexico, Land of Sunshine
      and Shadow.   Princeton: Van Nostrand, 1966.

616   Brand, Morton F. (pseud. Kaman al-Shimas).   Mexican
      Southland.   Fowler, Ind.:   Benton Review Shop, 1922.

617   Brasch, Rudolph.   Mexico, a Country of Contrasts.
      New York: D. McKay, 1967; London: Longmans,
      1968.

618   Brasher, Christopher.   Mexico 1968:   A Diary of the
      XIXth Olympiad.   London: S. Paul, 1968.

619   Brett, Dorothy Eugénie.   Lawrence and Brett: A
      Friendship.   London: M. Secker, 1933; Philadelphia:
      Lippincott, 1933.
      Memoirs of the English painter's relationship with
      D.H. Lawrence, including her visit to Oaxaca in
      1924.

620   Briggs, Lloyd Vernon.   Arizona and New Mexico, 1882;
      California, 1886; Mexico, 1891.   Boston: 1932.

621   Bright, Elizabeth Parks.   How about Mexico?   Boston:
      Chapman & Grimes, 1944.

622   Bright, Roderick.   The Land and People of Mexico.
      London: A & C Black, 1958; New York: Macmillan,
      1958.

623   Brine, Lindesay.   Travels amongst American Indians,
      Their Ancient Earthworks and Temples; Including a

Journey in Guatemala, Mexico, and Yucatan, and a Visit to the Ruins of Patinamit, Utatlan, Palenque, and Uxmal. London: J. Murray, 1883.

Brooks, Justus. See Barber, A.W.

624 Browne, John Ross. Adventures in the Apache Country: A Tour through Arizona and Sonora, with Notes on the Silver Regions of Nevada. New York: Harper, 1869.

625 Bruell, James D. Sea Memories, or Personal Experiences in the U.S. Navy in Peace and War. Biddeford Pool, Me.: 1886.
Memoirs, including experiences in Mexican-American War.

626 Bryant, William Cullen. Prose Writings, ed. Parke Godwin. V. 2. New York: D. Appleton, 1884.
"A Visit to Mexico" (letters): account of the American poet and editor's visit to Mexico City in 1872 at the invitation of the government.

627 Buck, Robert, and Robert F. Nixon. Battling the Elements. New York: G.P. Putnam's, 1934.
Account for young readers of two airplane flights, one from New York City to Mexico City, the second within the country.

628 Buffum, Edward Gould. Six Months in the Gold Mines: From a Journal of Three Years' Residence in Upper and Lower California, 1847-8-9. London: R. Bentley, 1850; Philadelphia: Lea & Blanchard, 1850.

629 Buhoup, Jonathan W. Narrative of the Central Division, or Army of Chihuahua, Commanded by Brigadier General Wool; Embracing All the Occurrences from the Time of Its Rendezvous at San Antonio de Bexar til Its Juncture with Gen'l Taylor and Its Final Disbandment at Camargo.... Pittsburgh: M.P. Morse, 1847.

630 Buick, Harry Arthur. The Gringoes of Tepehuanes. London: Longmans, 1967.

631 Bull, James Hunter. Journey of James H. Bull, Baja California, October 1843 to January 1844, ed. Doyce Blackman Nunis, Jr. Los Angeles: Dawson's Book Shop, 1965.

632   Bullock, William. Six Months' Residence and Travels
      in Mexico; Containing Remarks on the Present State
      of New Spain, Its Natural Productions, State of Society,
      Manufactures, Trade, Agriculture, and Antiquities.
      London: J. Murray, 1824.

      Bullock, W. H. See Hall, W. H. B.

633   Burbank, Addison. Mexican Frieze. New York:
      Coward-McCann, 1940.
            Account of visits to Indian villages made by the
            American author-illustrator. See also 76.

634   Burriss, Charles Walker. From New York to San
      Francisco by Way of Panama Canal Zone and All
      Central American Ports of the Pacific Ocean. Kansas
      City, Mo.: 1911.

635   Burroughs, William Seward (pseud. William Lee).
      Junkie. New York: Ace, 1953.
            Fictionalized memoirs, including account of the
            years spent by the American writer in Mexico City
            in the early 1950's. See also 79-80.

636   Bush, Ira Jefferson. Gringo Doctor. Caldwell, Id.:
      Caxton, 1939.
            Autobiography, including account of the Texan
            doctor's experiences in the Mexican Revolution.

637   Bush, Wesley A. Paradise to Leeward: Cruising the
      West Coast of Mexico. New York: Van Nostrand,
      1954.
            Account of a cruise from Los Angeles to Acapulco
            and handbook.

638   Bynner, Witter. Journey with Genius: Recollections
      and Reflections Concerning the D. H. Lawrences. New
      York: J. Day, 1951; London: P. Nevill, 1953.
            Memoirs by the American poet of his visit to Mexi-
            co City and Chapala with the Lawrences in 1923.
            See also 83-85.

      Caddy, John Herbert. See Pendergast, D. M.

639   Calderón de la Barca, Frances Erskine Inglis. (a) Life
      in Mexico during a Residence of Two Years in That

Country. Boston: Little, Brown, 1843; London: Chapman & Hall, 1843. (b) Life in Mexico: The Letters of Fanny Calderón de la Barca with New Material from the Author's Private Journals, ed. Howard T. and Marion Hall Fisher. Garden City: Doubleday, 1966.
> Letters by the Scottish-American wife of the first Spanish ambassador, describing their life in the capital 1839-1842. See also 1148.

640 Cameron, Charlotte Wales-Almy. Mexico in Revolution: An Account of an English Woman's Experiences & Adventures in the Land of Revolution, with a Description of the People, the Beauties of the Country & the Highly Interesting Remains of Aztec Civilization. London: Seeley, 1925.

641 Campbell, Reau. Mexico and the Mexicans: The Material Matters and Mysterious Myths of That Country and Its People. México: Sonora News, 1892.

642 Canfield, Delos Lincoln. East Meets West, South of the Border: Essays on Spanish American Life and Attitudes. Carbondale: Southern Illinois University, 1968.
> "Excursions to Mexico."

643 Cannon, Raymond, and others. The Sea of Cortez. Menlo Park, Calif.: Lane Magazine, 1966.
> Description of the Gulf of California.

644 Carbutt, Mary Rhodes (Mrs. E. H. Carbutt). Five Months' Fine Weather in Canada, Western U.S., and Mexico. London: S. Low, etc., 1889.

645 Cardif, Maurice (pseud. John Lincoln). One Man's Mexico: A Record of Travels and Encounters. London: Bodley Head, 1967; New York: Harcourt, Brace & World, 1968.
> Account of travel between 1958 and 1964 by the English author.

646 Carnes, Cecil, and Fred Carnes. You Must Go to Mexico.... Chicago: Ziff-Davis, 1947.
> Account of a trip down the Pan-American highway made by the two American journalists.

647 Carpenter, Frank George. Mexico. Garden City:
     Doubleday, 1924.
     Description, part of a series.

648 Carpenter, William W. Travels and Adventures in
     Mexico, in the Course of Journeys of Upward of 2500
     Miles Performed on Foot...., New York: Harper,
     1851.

649 Carr, Harry. Old Mother Mexico. Boston: Houghton
     Mifflin, 1931.
     Account of a trip made by the American journalist.

650 Carson, Christopher. Kit Carson's Own Story of His
     Life..., ed. Blanche Chloe Grant. Taos: 1926.
     Autobiography, including an account of the moun-
     tainman's experiences in New Mexico.

651 Carson, William English. (a) Mexico, the Wonderland
     of the South. New York: Macmillan, 1909. (b) 2nd
     ed. New York: Macmillan, 1914.
     Description and interpretation of present-day condi-
     tions.

652 Carter, Pel. Trails and Tales of Baja. Lake San
     Marcos, Calif.: Southwest Arts, 1967.

653 Case, Alden Buell. Thirty Years with the Mexicans in
     Peace and Revolution. New York: F.H. Revell, 1917.

654 Castaneda, Carlos. Journey to Ixtlan: The Lessons of
     Don Juan. New York: Simon & Schuster, 1972.

655 _____. A Separate Reality: Further Conversations
     with Don Juan. New York: Simon & Schuster, 1971.

656 _____. The Teachings of Don Juan: A Yaqui Way
     of Knowledge. Berkeley: University of California,
     1968; Harmondsworth, Eng.: Penguin, 1970.
     Three memoirs [654-6] of the American Anthropol-
     ogist's association with a Yaqui Indian brujo.

657 Catherwood, Frederick. Views of Ancient Monvments
     in Central America, Chiapas, and Yvcatan. London:
     F. Catherwood, 1844; New York: Bartlett & Welford,
     1844.

Essay and illustrations of Maya ruins by the English architect, who accompanied John Lloyd Stephens on his two expeditions.

658   Cerwin, Herbert. These Are the Mexicans. New York: Reynal & Hitchcock, 1947.
      Interpretation of present conditions by the Mexican-born American.

659   Chamberlain, George Agnew. Is Mexico Worth Saving? Indianapolis: Bobbs-Merrill, 1920.
      Interpretation of present conditions by the former American consul-general to Mexico City. See also 91-92.

660   Chamberlain, Samuel Emory. My Confession, Written and Illustrated by Samuel E. Chamberlain, ed. Roger Butterfield. New York: Harper, 1956.
      Memoirs, with illustrations, of the American author's experiences during the Mexican-American War.

      Chandos, Dane. See Lilley, P.

661   Chase, Stuart, and Marian Tyler. Mexico: A Study of Two Americas. New York: Macmillan, 1931; London: J. Lane, 1932.
      Comparison of Tepoztlán with "Middletown."

      Chilton, John. See Hakluyt, R.

662   Church, John H.C. Diary of a Trip through Mexico and California. Pittsfield, Mass.: M.H. Rogers, 1887.

663   Clark, Leonard Francis. Yucatan Adventure. London: Hutchinson, 1959.

664   Clarke, A.B. Travels in Mexico and California; Comprising a Journal of a Tour from Brazos Santiago through Central Mexico by Way of Monterey, Chihuahua, the Country of the Apaches, and the River Gila, to the Mining Districts of California. Boston: Wright & Hasty, 1852.

      Cleveland, June. See Lamb, D.

665 Cleveland, Richard Jeffry. In the Forecastle, or Twenty-Five Years a Sailor. New York: Hurst, 1843.

666 Coffin, Alfred Oscar. Land without Chimneys, or The
Byways of Mexico. Cincinnati: Editor, 1898.

667 Cohn, Dorothy Dell. Down Mexico Way. San Antonio:
Naylor, 1958.

668 Coit, Daniel Wadsworth. Digging for Gold without a
Shovel: The Letters of Daniel Wadsworth Coit from
Mexico City to San Francisco, 1848-1851, ed. George
P. Hammond. Denver: Old West, 1967.

Coleman, Barb. See Arthur, J.

669 Colton, Walter. Three Years in California (1846-1849).
New York: A.S. Barnes, 1850.

670 Conkling, Howard. Mexico and the Mexicans, or Notes
of Travel in the Winter and Spring of 1883. New
York: Taintor, Merrill, 1883.

671 The Conquest of Santa Fé and Subjugation of New Mexico
by the Military Forces of the United States ... and a
History of Colonel Doniphan's Campaign in Chihuahua;
by a Captain of Volunteers. Philadelphia: H. Packer,
1847.

Conrad, David Holmes. See McSherry, R.

672 Cook, James. Remarks on a Passage from the River
Balise, in the Bay of Honduras, to Merida, the Capi-
tal of the Province of Jucatan in the Spanish West
Indies. London: C. Parker, 1769.

673 Cooke, Edward. A Voyage to the South Seas and Round
the World, Perform'd in the Years 1708, 1709, 1710,
and 1711...; A Description of the American Coasts
from Tierra del Fuego in the South to California in
the North... London: B. Lintot & R. Gosling, 1712.

674 Cooke, Philip St. George. The Conquest of New Mexico and California: An Historical and Personal Narrative. New York: G.P. Putnam's, 1878.

675 Corney, Peter. Voyages in the Northern Pacific: Narrative of Several Trading Voyages from 1813 to 1818 between the North West Coast of America, the Hawaiian Islands, and China... Honolulu: T.C. Thrum, 1896.

676 Couts, Cave Johnson. Hepah, California! The Journal ... from Monterey, Nuevo Leon, Mexico, to Los Angeles, California, during the Years 1848-1849, ed. Henry F. Dobyns. Tucson: Arizona Pioneers Historical Society, 1961.

Coyner, David Holmes. See 107.

677 Crane, (Harold) Hart. Letters, 1916-1932, ed. Brom Weber. New York: Hermitage House, 1952.
The American poet lived in Mexico City and Taxco 1931-1932. See also 108.

678 Crane, Stephen. (a) Uncollected Writings, ed. Olov W. Fryckstedt. Uppsala, Sweden: University of Uppsala, 1963. (b) Stephen Crane in the West and Mexico, ed. Joseph Katz. Kent, O.: Kent State University, 1970. (a-b) "Mexican Sights and Street Scenes," "Free Silver Down in Mexico," "Ancient Capital of Montezuma," "Jugs of Pulque Down in Mexico," "Hats, Shirts, and Spurs in Mexico"; (b) "The main streets of this city," "The Viga Canal," and "Above all things" (newspaper articles): the American writer visited Mexico City and southern Mexico in 1895. See also 109-110.

679 Crawford, Cora Hayward. The Land of the Montezumas. New York: J.B. Alden, 1889.

Crawford, Oswald. See Harris, W.R.

680 Creuzbaur, Robert. Route from the Gulf of Mexico and the Lower Mississippi Valley to California and the Pacific Ocean. New York: 1849.

681 Croffut, William Augustus. Folks Next Door: The Log Book of a Rambler. Washington: Eastside, 1904.

682 Crow, John Armstrong. Mexico Today. New York: Harper, 1957.
Interpretation of present-day conditions.

683 Dame, Lawrence. Yucatan. New York: Random House,
     1941; London: V. Gollancz, 1942.
     Account of a visit made by the American journalist.

684 Dampier, William. A New Voyage round the World;
     Describing ... the South Sea Coasts of Chili, Peru,
     and Mexico.... London: J. Knapton, 1697.

685 Dana, Richard Henry Jr. (a) Two Years before the
     Mast: A Personal Narrative of Life at Sea. Boston:
     Houghton Mifflin, 1840; London: E. Moxon, 1840 (?).
     (b) Two Years before the Mast: A Personal Narrative
     of Life at Sea; Edited from the Original Manuscript
     and from the First Edition, with Journals and Letters
     of 1834-36 and 1859-60, by John Haskell Kemble.
     Los Angeles: W. Ritchie, 1964.
     Account of the American author's 1835-1836 cruise
     along the California coast.

686 Daniels, Josephus. Shirt-Sleeve Diplomat. Chapel Hill:
     University of North Carolina, 1947.
     Memoirs by the American ambassador, 1933-1942.

687 Davis, William Heath. Sixty Years in California: A
     History of Events in California--Personal, Political,
     and Military--under the Mexican Regime, during the
     Quasi-Military Government of the Territory by the
     United States, and after the Admission of the State
     into the Union; Being a Compilation by a Witness of
     the Events Described. San Francisco: A.J. Leary,
     1889.

688 Davis, William Watts Hart. El Gringo, or New Mexi-
     co and Her People. New York: Harper, 1857.

689 Del Villar, Mary, and Fred Del Villar. Where the
     Strange Roads Go Down. New York: 1953.
     Account of a walking trip through Michoacan in
     1951.

690 Dewees, William B. Letters from an Early Settler of
     Texas, ed. Eimaretta C. Kimball. Louisville: Morton
     & Griswold, 1852.

691 Dewey, John. Impressions of Soviet Russia and the
     Revolutionary World: Mexico--China--Turkey. New
     York: New Republic, 1929.

"Church and State in Mexico," "Mexico's Educational Renaissance," "From a Mexican Notebook," and "Imperialism Is Easy" (articles): the American educator was in Mexico City in 1926.

692 Diamant, Gertrude. The Days of Ofelia. Boston: Houghton Mifflin, 1942; London: Hurst & Blackett, 1942.
Description of the life of a ten-year-old Indian girl, the American ethnologist's maid.

693 Dickerson, Grace Leslie. Sketchbook of San Miguel de Allende. New York: Vantage, 1964.

Dickinson, Stirling. See Bowman, H.

694 Dobie, James Frank. Some Part of Myself. Boston: Little, Brown, 1967.
Autobiography, one section dealing with his trips into northern Mexico in the 1930's. See also 127-128.

695 _____. Tongues of the Monte. Garden City: Doubleday, 1935. Tongues of the Monte: The Mexico I Like... London: Hammond, Hammond, 1948.
Memoirs of expeditions into northern Mexico by horseback made in the early 1930's. One American edition was entitled The Mexico I Like.

696 Dodge, David. How Green Was My Father: A Sort of Travel Diary. New York: Simon & Schuster, 1947; London: Home & Van Thal, 1950.
Account of an automobile trip through Mexico to Guatemala.

697 Donaldson, Stuart Alexander. Mexico Thirty Years Ago, as Described in a Series of Private Letters by a Youth. London: W.R. Gray, 1866.

698 Donnavan, Corydon. Adventures in Mexico Experienced during a Captivity of Seven Months in the Interior-- Having Been Captured at Camargo by Canales' Band of Guerillas and Sold into Slavery, Final Excape and Perilous Journey to the United States--with a View of the Present War. Cincinnati: Robinson & Jones, 1847.

699 Dos Passos, John Roderigo. In All Countries. London: Constable, 1934; New York: Harcourt, Brace, 1934.

"Relief Map of Mexico," "Zapata's Ghost Walks,"
and "Emiliano Zapata" (articles): the American
novelist visited the capital and Morelos in 1926
and probably 1932. See also 129.

700 Downing, Todd. The Mexican Earth. New York: Doubleday, Doran, 1940.
Description and interpretation of present-day conditions. See also 130-133.

701 Drees, Charles William. Thirteen Years in Mexico
(From Letters of Charles W. Drees), ed. Ada M.C.
Drees. New York: Abingdon, 1915.

702 Dunn, Robert. World Alive: A Personal Story. New
York: Crown, 1956; London: R. Hale, 1958.
Autobiography, including accounts of his experiences
during the invasion of Veracruz in 1914 and with
the Pershing expedition of 1916.

703 Duval, B.R. A Narrative of Life and Travels in Mexico and British Honduras. Boston: 1881. [From
Gardiner]

Duval, John Crittenden. See 140.

704 Dye, Job Francis. Recollections of a Pioneer, 1830-
1852. Los Angeles: 1951.
Memoirs of an American settler in California.

705 Eccleston, Robert. Overland to California on the South-
western Trail, 1849: Diary of Robert Eccleston, ed.
George P. Hammond and Edward H. Howes. Berkeley:
University of California, 1950.

706 Edwards, Frank S. A Campaign in New Mexico with
Colonel Doniphan. Philadelphia: Carey & Hart, 1847.

Edwards, Marcellus Ball. See Bieber, R.P.

707 Edwards, William Seymour. On the Mexican Highlands,
with a Passing Glimpse of Cuba. Cincinnati: Jennings
& Graham, 1906.

708 Elderkin, James D. Biographical Sketches and Anecdotes of a Soldier of Three Wars, as Written by

Himself: The Florida, the Mexican War, and the
Great Rebellion, Together with Sketches of Travel....
Detroit: Record, 1899.

709 Elton, James Frederick. With the French in Mexico.
London: Chapman & Hall, 1867.

710 Encarnacion Prisoners; Comprising an Account of the
March of the Kentucky Cavalry from Louisville to the
Rio Grande, Together with an Authentic History of the
Captivity of the American Prisoners, Including Inci-
dents and Sketches of Men and Things on the Route
and in Mexico; by a Prisoner. Louisville: Prentice
& Weissinger, 1848.

711 Eskelund, Karl. Kælighedens kaktus: En skildring fra
Mexiko. København: Gyldendal, 1955. The Cactus of
Love: Travels in Mexico. London: A. Redman,
1957; New York: Taplinger, 1961.
Account of a visit made by the Danish author and
his Chinese wife.

712 Eudaly, Marie Saddler. Dickie in Mexico. Nashville:
Broadman, 1951.

713 Evans, Albert S. Our Sister Republic: A Gala Trip
through Tropical Mexico in 1869-70: Adventures and
Sight-Seeing in the Land of the Aztecs, with Picturesque Descriptions of the Country and the People and
Reminiscences of the Empire and Its Downfall. Hart-
ford: Columbian, 1870; Toledo, O.: W. E. Bliss,
1870.

714 Evans, George W. B. Mexican Gold Trail: The Journal
of a Forty-Niner, ed. Glenn S. Dumke. San Marino,
Calif.: Huntington Library, 1945.

715 Evans, Rosalie Caden. The Rosalie Evans Letters from
Mexico, ed. Daisy Caden Pettus. Indianapolis: Bobbs-
Merrill, 1926; London: Hodder & Stoughton, 1926.
Letters by the American widow of an English owner
of an hacienda, which the Mexicans wanted to ex-
propriate, giving an account of her resistance until
her murder in 1924.

716 Falconer, Thomas. Expedition to Santa Fe: An Account of Its Journey from Texas through Mexico with

Particulars of Its Capture. New Orleans: 1842.

717 Farham, Thomas Jefferson. Mexico: Its Geography,
Its People, and Its Institutions, with a Map Containing
the Result of the Latest Explorations of Fremont,
Wilkes, and Others. New York: H. Long, 1846.

718 _____. Travels in the Californias and Scenes in the
Pacific Ocean. New York: Saxton & Miles, 1844.

719 Farrell, James Thomas. Reflections at Fifty, and
Other Essays. New York: Vanguard, 1954.
"Dewey in Mexico": account of John Dewey's return to Mexico City in 1937 to head an inquiry
about Leon Trotsky.

Ferguson, Philip Gooch. See Bieber, R. P.

720 Fergusson, Erna. Fiesta in Mexico. New York: Knopf,
1934.
Account of a visit made by the American author to
seek out Indian fiestas.

721 _____. Mexico Revisited. New York: Knopf, 1955.
Account of an automobile trip made from Texas to
Yucatán.

722 Ferlinghetti, Lawrence. The Mexican Night: Travel
Journal. New York: New Directions, 1970.
Notes from several trips, mostly made in the 1960's,
to Baja California, Yucatán, and San Miguel de
Allende.

723 Field, Matthew C. Mott. Field on the Santa Fe Trail,
ed. John E. Sanders from materials collected by
Clyde and Mae Reed Porter. Norman: University of
Oklahoma, 1960.
Articles and a journal in verse from the American
editor's 1839 visit to New Mexico.

724 Flandrau, Charles Macomb. Loquacities. New York,
London: D. Appleton, 1931.
"Of Earthquakes" and "Jarana at Breakfast" (es-
says).

725 _____. Viva Mexico! New York: D. Appleton,
1908.

Essays about life on his brother's coffee plantation
near Misantla and visits to Puebla, Mexico City,
and Cuernavaca, as seen by the American author
between 1903 and 1908. See also 151.

726 Flippin, John R. Sketches from the Mountains of Mexico. Cincinnati: Standard, 1889.

727 Folsom, George. Mexico in 1842: A Description of the
Country, Its Natural and Political Features, with a
Sketch of Its History Brought Down to the Present
Year, to Which Is Added an Account of Texas and
Yucatan and of the Santa Fé Expedition. New York:
C.J. Folsom, 1842.

728 Fonville, Nina. Hold Fast These Earth-Warm Stones.
San Antonio: Naylor, 1949.

729 Forbes, [?]. Trip to Mexico, or Recollections of
a Ten-Months' Ramble in 1849-50; by a Barrister.
London: Smith, Elder, 1851.

730 Ford, Isaac Nelson. Tropical America. New York:
Scribners, 1893.

731 Ford, Norman D. Lands in the Sun. Greenlawn, N.Y.:
Harian, 1950.

732 Foster, Harry La Tourette. A Gringo in Mañana-Land.
London: J. Lane, 1924; New York: Dodd, Mead,
1924.
Account of two visits made by the American journalist in 1919 and the early 1920's.

733 Foster, John Watson. Diplomatic Memoirs. Boston:
Houghton Mifflin, 1909.

734 Foulke, William Dudley. Protean Papers. New York,
London: Putnam's, 1903.
"On Mexican Mountains" and "A Visit to Yucatan"
(essays). See also 157-158.

735 _____. A Random Record of Travel during Fifty
Years. New York: Oxford University, 1925.

736 Fraenkel, Michael. Land of the Quetzal: Excerpts
from The Journal (the Mexican Years, 1940-1944).
Yonkers: D. Baradinsky, 1946.

737   Franck, Alzina B. A Jaunt by Mexican Bus: An Un-
      common Travel Book for the Young in Heart. New
      York: Exposition, 1960.

738   Franck, Harry Alverson. Trailing Cortez through
      Mexico. New York: F.A. Stokes, 1935.
      Account of a walking tour along Cortés's route.

739   _____. Tramping through Mexico, Guatemala, and
      Honduras; Being the Random Notes of an Incurable
      Vagabond. London: T. Fisher, 1916; New York:
      Century, 1916.
      Account of a trip made in 1911, starting at the
      Texas border.

740   _____, and Herbert C. Lanks. The Pan American
      Highway from the Rio Grande to the Canal Zone. New
      York, London: Appleton-Century, 1940.
      Description of life along the highway.

741   Frank, Waldo David. America Hispana: A Portrait
      and a Prospect. New York: Scribner's, 1931; London:
      Scribner's, 1932.
      Chapter provides description and interpretation of
      present situation, based upon the American novelist's
      1929 visit.

742   Frémont, John Charles. (a) Report of the Exploring
      Expedition to the Rocky Mountains in the Year 1842
      and to Oregon and North California in the Years 1843-
      '44. Washington: Blair & Rives, 1845; London:
      1846. (b) The Expeditions of John Charles Frémont.
      V. 1: Travels from 1838 to 1844, ed. Donald Jackson
      and Mary Lee Spence. Urbana: University of Illinois,
      1970.

743   Funnell, William. A Voyage round the World; Contain-
      ing an Account of Captain Dampier's Expedition into
      the South Seas in the Ship St. George in the Years
      1703 and 1704, Together with the Author's Voyage
      from Amapalla on the West Coast of Mexico to East
      India. London: W. Botham, 1707.

744   Furber, George C. The Twelve Months Volunteer, or
      Journal of a Private in the Tennessee Regiment of
      Cavalry in the Campaign in Mexico, 1846-7, Compris-
      ing Four General Subjects: I. A Soldier's Life in

Camp: Amusements, Duties, Hardships; II. A De-
scription of Texas and Mexico as Seen on the March;
III. Manners, Customs, Religious Ceremonies of the
Mexicans; IV. The Operation of All the Twelve Months
Volunteers, Including a Complete History of the War
with Mexico. Cincinnati: J.A. & A.P. James, 1848.

745 Fyfe, Henry Hamilton. The Real Mexico: A Study on
the Spot. London: W. Heinemann, 1914; New York:
McBride, Nast, 1914.
Description and interpretation of present conditions,
made by an English journalist.

746 Gadow, Hans Frederich. Through Southern Mexico;
Being an Account of the Travels of a Naturalist.
London: Witherby, 1908; New York: Scribner's, 1908.
Account of two visits made in 1902 and 1904.

747 Gage, Thomas. The English-American: His Travail by
Sea and Land, or A New Svrvey of the West-India's;
Containing a Journall of Three Thousand and Three
Hundred Miles within the Main Land of America.
London: R. Cotes, 1648.
Memoirs of life in Mexico 1625-1627 and in Guate-
mala, and the first survey of the area ever written.
The English author was a priest in a Spanish order.

748 Galarza, Ernesto. Barrio Boy. Notre Dame: University of Notre Dame, 1971.
Autobiography by an American, including account of
life in Mexico.

749 Gann, Thomas William Francis. Ancient Cities and
Modern Tribes: Explorations and Adventure in Maya
Land. London: Duckworth, 1926; New York:
Scribner's, 1926.

750 _____. In an Unknown Land. London: Duckworth,
1924.

751 _____. Maya Cities: A Record of Exploration and
Adventure in Middle America. London: Duckworth,
1927.
Three memoirs [749-51] about expeditions made by
the English archaeologist.

752   Gardner, Erle Stanley. The Hidden Heart of Baja.
      New York: Morrow, 1962; London: Jarrolds, 1964.

753   _____ . Host with the Big Hat. New York: Morrow,
      1969.

754   _____ . Hovering over Baja. New York: Morrow,
      1961.

755   _____ . Hunting the Desert Whale: Personal Adven-
      ture in Baja California. New York: Morrow, 1960;
      London: Jarrolds, 1963.

756   _____ . The Land of Shorter Shadows. New York:
      W. Thomas, 1948.

757   _____ . Mexico's Magic Square. New York: W.
      Morrow, 1968.

758   _____ . Neighborhood Frontiers: Desert Country,
      Puget Sound Country, Yucatan Peninsula, Yaqui River,
      Barranca Country. New York: Morrow, 1954.

759   _____ . Off the Beaten Track in Baja. New York:
      Morrow, 1967.
      Accounts of visits [all but 758] to Baja California
      and the Gulf of California, made by the American
      mystery writer.

760   Garner, Bess Adams. Mexico: Notes in the Margin.
      Boston: Houghton Mifflin, 1937.
      Account of visits made by the American theater di-
      rector.

761   Garner, William Robert. Letters from California, 1845-
      1847, ed. Donald Munns Craig. Berkeley: University
      of California, 1970.

762   Geiger, John Lewis. A Peep at Mexico: Narrative of
      a Journey across the Republic from the Pacific to the
      Gulf in December 1873 and January 1874. London:
      Trübner, 1874.

763   Geiger, Maynard J. The Sierra Trail in Picture and
      Story. Santa Barbara: Franciscan Fathers of Cali-
      fornia, 1960.

764 George, Alfred. Holidays at Home and Abroad. London: W.J. Johnson, 1877.

765 Gessler, Clifford. Pattern of Mexico. New York, London: Appleton-Century, 1941.
Account of travels made by the American author.

766 Gibson, George Rutledge. Journal of a Soldier under Kearney and Doniphan, 1846-1847, ed. Ralph Paul Bieber. Glendale, Calif.: A.H. Clark, 1935.

767 Giddings, Luther. Sketches of the Campaign in Northern Mexico in Eighteen Hundred Forty-Six and Seven; by an Officer of the First Regiment of Ohio Volunteers. New York: G.P. Putnam, 1853.

768 Gilliam, Albert M. Travels over the Table Lands and Cordilleras of Mexico during the Years 1843 and 44, including a Description of California.... Philadelphia: J.W. Moore, 1846; Aberdeen: 1847.

769 Gillpatrick, Owen Wallace. The Man Who Likes Mexico: The Spirited Chronicle of Adventurous Wanderings in Mexican Highways and Byways. New York: Century, 1911. Wanderings in Mexico: The Spirited Chronicle of Adventure in Mexican Highways and Byways. London: E. Nash, 1912.
Account of six years' travel made by the American businessman turned wanderer.

770 Gilpin, Laura. Temples in Yucatan: A Camera Chronicle of Chichén Itzá. New York: Hastings House, 1948.

771 Gipson, Frederick Benjamin. "The Cow Killers": With the Aftosa Commission in Mexico. Austin: University of Texas, 1956.
Anecdotes about the work to eradicate hoof-and-mouth disease.

772 Gleason, Joe Duncan, and Dorothy Gleason. Sketches and Paintings from Mexico. N.p.: 1963.

773 Godoy, Mercedes. When I Was a Girl in Mexico. Boston: Lothrop, Lee & Shepard, 1919.
Memoir, written for children.

774   Goertz, Arthémise.   South of the Border.   New York:
      Macmillan, 1940; London: Jarrolds, 1941.
      Account of a visit to small towns, partly fictional.

      Gooch, Fanny Chambers.   See Iglehart, F. C. G.

775   Goodhue, Bertram Grosvenor.   Mexican Memories:
      The Record of a Slight Sojourn below the Yellow Rio
      Grande.   New York: G. M. Allen, 1892.

776   Goodspeed, Bernice I.   Criada.   México: 1950.

777   Goodwin, Joseph Carl.   Through Mexico on Horseback:
      Forty Days and Forty Nights in the Wilderness of Old
      Mexico.   Dallas: South-West, 1933.

778   Graham, Stephen.   In Quest of El Dorado.   New York:
      D. Appleton, 1923; London: Macmillan, 1924.
      Account of a trip through the West Indies, the
      United States, Mexico, and Central America which
      retraced the routes of the Spanish explorers.

779   Grant, Ulysses Simpson.   Personal Memoirs of U. S.
      Grant.   New York: C. L. Webster, 1885-1886.
      Autobiography, including an account of the Amer-
      ican statesman's role in the Mexican-American
      War.

780   Gray, Albert Zabriskie.   Mexico as It Is; Being Notes
      of a Recent Tour in That Country, with Some Practical
      Information for Travellers in That Direction, as Also
      Some Study on the Church Question.   New York: E. P.
      Dutton, 1878.

781   Greene, Graham.   The Lawless Roads: A Mexican
      Journey.   London: Longmans, Green, 1939.   Another
      Mexico.   New York: Viking, 1939.
      Account of a trip made from Texas to Chiapas in
      1938.   See also 190-191.

782   Gregg, Josiah.   Commerce of the Prairies, or The
      Journal of a Santa Fé Trader during Eight Expeditions
      across the Great Western Prairies and a Residence
      of Nearly Nine Years in Northern Mexico.   New York:
      H. G. Langley, 1844.
      Account of life in New Mexico as witnessed by the
      American trader between 1831 and 1841.

783 _____ . Diaries & Letters..., ed. Maurice Garland
Fulton. Norman: University of Oklahoma, 1941-1944.

784 Grey, Edward. Twenty-Five Years, 1892-1916. Lon-
don: Hodder & Stoughton, 1925; New York: F.A.
Stokes, 1925.
Memoirs by the English diplomat.

785 Grey, Zane. Tales of Southern Rivers. London: Hodder & Stoughton, 1924; New York, London: Harper,
1924.
"Down an Unknown Jungle River": account of an
expedition above Tampico made by the American
writer of westerns in 1911. See also 195-196.

786 Griffin, Solomon Bulkley. Mexico of To-day. New
York: Harper, 1886.

787 Gunn, Lewis Carstairs, and Elizabeth Le Breton Gunn.
Records of a California Family: Journals and Letters..., ed. Anna Lee Marston. San Diego: 1928.

788 Gunther, John. Inside Latin America. New York:
Harper, 1941; London: H. Hamilton, 1942.
Chapter provides description and interpretation of
present situation, based upon the American author's
visit in 1940.

789 Guthrie, Patty. Eliza and Etheldreda in Mexico: Notes
of Travel. New York: Broadway, 1911.

790 Gutiérrez de Lara, Lázaro, and Edgcumb Pinchon. The
Mexican People: Their Struggle for Freedom. Garden
City: Doubleday, Page, 1914; London: C. Brown,
1914.
Interpretation of the present situation from the
Revolutionaries' side, written by a Mexican and an
American.

791 Hager, Anna Marie, ed. The Filibusters of 1890: The
Captain John F. Janes and Lower California Newspaper
Reports and the Walter G. Smith Manuscript. Los
Angeles: Dawson's Book Shop, 1968.

792 Haggard, Henry Rider. The Days of My Life: An Autobiography, ed. Charles James Longman. London:
Longmans, Green, 1926.

Memoirs, including an account of his 1891 visit
with J. Gladwyn Jebb in Mexico City and Chiapas.
See also 200-201.

793 Hail, John B. To Mexico with Love: San Miguel with
Side Dishes. New York: Exposition, 1966.

794 Hakluyt, Richard, ed. The Principall Navigations,
Voiages, and Discoveries of the English Nation Made
by Sea or ouer Land... London: G. Bishop & R.
Newberie, 1589.
Memoirs by four merchants, Robert Tomson, who
was there between 1556 and 1561, Roger Bodenham,
1564-1565, John Chilton, 1568-1585, and Henrie
Hawks, five years sometime before 1572; by John
Hawkins (see 811); and by two survivors of his
voyage, Miles Philips, 1568-1582, and David Ingram,
1568.

795 Hall, Basil. Extracts from a Journal Written on the
Coasts of Chili, Peru, and Mexico in the Years 1820,
1821, 1822. Edinburgh: A. Constable, 1824; Philadelphia: E. Littell, 1824.
The author was a British captain.

796 Hall, William Henry Bullock (pseud. W. H. Bullock).
Across Mexico in 1864-5. London: Macmillan, 1866.

797 Halliburton, Richard. New Worlds to Conquer. Indianapolis: Bobbs-Merrill, 1929; London: G. Bles, 1930.
Account of the American adventurer's ascent of
Popocatépetl and dive into the pool at Chichén Itzá
in 1928.

798 Halpin, Will R. Two Men in the West. Pittsburgh:
Shaw, 1898.

799 Hamilton, Charles Walter. Early Day Oil Tales of
Mexico. Houston: Gulf, 1966.

800 Hamilton, William Thomas. My Sixty Years on the
Plains, Trapping, Trading, and Indian Fighting, ed.
E. T. Sieber. New York: Forest & Stream, 1905.

801 Hanley, May Carr. With John Brun in Old Mexico.
Mountain View, Calif.: Pacific, 1924.
See also 205.

802   Hanson, Paul M. In the Land of the Feathered Serpent.
      Independence, Mo.: Herald House, 1949.

803   Harding, George Canady. The Miscellaneous Writings...
      Indianapolis: Carlon & Hollenbeck, 1882.
      "Pencil Notes of a Brief Trip to Mexico."

804   Hardy, Robert William Hale. Travels in the Interior
      of Mexico in 1825, 1826, 1827, & 1828. London:
      H. Colburn & R. Bentley, 1829.

805   Harper, Henry Howard. A Journey in Southeastern
      Mexico: Narrative of Experiences and Observations
      on Agricultural and Industrial Conditions. Boston:
      De Vinne, 1910.

806   Harris, Benjamin Butler. The Gila Trail: The Texas
      Argonauts and the California Gold Rush, ed. Richard
      H. Dillon. Norman: University of Oklahoma, 1960.

807   Harris, William Richard. Days and Nights in the
      Tropics. Toronto: Morang, 1905.

808   _____ (pseud. Oswald Crawford). By Path and Trail.
      Salt Lake: Intermountain Catholic, 1908.

809   Hartman, George W. A Private's Own Journal; Giving
      an Account of the Battles of Mexico under Gen'l Scott,
      with Descriptive Scenes.... Greencastle, Pa.: E.
      Robinson, 1849.

810   Haven, Gilbert. Our Next Door Neighbor: A Winter in
      Mexico. New York: Harper, 1875.

      Hawkes, Onera Amelia Merritt. See Merritt-Hawkes,
      O.A.

811   Hawkins, John. A True Declaration of the Troublesome
      Voyadge of Mr. John Hawkins to the Parties of Guynea
      and the West Indies in the Yeares of Our Lord 1567
      and 1568. London: T. Purfoote, 1569.
         Account of the battle in the harbor of Veracruz from
      which Hawkins and Francis Drake had to flee.

      Hawks, Henrie. See Hakluyt, R.

      Hedges, Frederick Albert Mitchell. See Mitchell-
      Hedges, F.A.

812   Henry, William Seaton. Campaign Sketches of the War
      with Mexico. New York: Harper, 1847.

813   Hill, Emma Shepard. Doing Mexico with James. Den-
      ver: Bradford-Robinson, 1924.

814   Hill, S.S. Travels in Peru and Mexico. London:
      Longmans, Green, etc., 1860.

815   Hilton, John W. Sonora Sketch Book. New York: Mac-
      millan, 1947.
          Memoirs about eight years in northern Mexico.

816   Hilton, William Hayes. Sketches in the Southwest and
      Mexico, 1858-1877, ed. Corey S. Bliss. Los Angeles:
      Dawson's Bookshop, 1963.

817   Hobbs, James. Wild Life in the Far West: Personal
      Adventures of a Border Mountain Man; Comprising
      Hunting and Trapping Adventures with Kit Carson and
      Others, Captivity and Life among the Comanches,
      Services under Doniphan in the War with Mexico, and
      in the Mexican War against the French.... Hartford:
      Wiley, Waterman & Eaton, 1872.

818   Hogner, Dorothy Childs. South to Padre. Boston:
      Lothrop, Lee & Shepard, 1936.
          Account of a trip made with her husband to Texas
      and Mexico in 1935. See also 226.

819   Holbrook, Anna Jane. Come Down Some Time: An
      American Housewife South of the Border. New York:
      Exposition, 1955.

820   Holley, Mary Austin. Texas: Observations--Historical,
      Geographical, and Descriptive--in a Series of Letters
      Written during a Visit to Austin's Colony, with a
      View of a Permanent Settlement in That Country, in
      the Autumn of 1831. Baltimore: Armstrong &
      Plaskitt, 1833.

821   Hornaday, William Temple. Camp-Fires on Desert and
      Lava. London: T.W. Laurie, 1908; New York:
      Scribner's, 1909.

822   Horton, Inez. Copper's Children: The Rise and Fall
      of a Mexican Copper Mining Camp. New York: Ex-
      position, 1968.

823 Hortop, Job. The Rare Trauailes of Iob Hortop, an
Englishman Who Was Not Heard of in Three and
Twentie Yeeres Space.... London: W. Wright, 1591.
Memoirs by a survivor of the Hawkins voyage of
1568.

824 Houston, Samuel. The Writings of Sam Houston, 1813-
1863, ed. Amelia W. Williams and Eugene Campbell
Barker. Austin: University of Texas, 1938-1943.
Materials from an early American settler of Texas.

825 Howard of Glossop, Winifred Mary De Lisle. Journal
of a Tour in the United States, Canada, and Mexico.
London: S. Low, Marston, 1897.

826 Hughes, (James) Langston. The Big Sea: An Autobiography. New York: Knopf, 1940; London, Melbourne:
Hutchinson, 1941.
Memoir, including an account of the American poet's
life in Toluca with his father 1919-1921. See also
233.

827 _____. I Wonder as I Wander: An Autobiographical
Journey. New York: Rinehart, 1956.
Memoir, including an account of his Bohemian life
in Mexico City 1934-1935.

828 Hughes, John Taylor. Doniphan's Expedition; Containing
an Account of His Conquest of New Mexico, General
Kearney's Overland Expedition to California, Doniphan's
Campaign against the Navajos, His Unparalleled March
upon Chihuahua and Durango, and the Operations of
General Price at Santa Fe. Cincinnati: J.S. & U.P.
James, 1848.

829 Hulbert, Archer Butler, ed. Southwest on the Turquoise
Trail: The First Diaries on the Road to Santa Fe...,
1810-1825. Colorado Springs: 1933.

830 Humphrey, Zephine. 'Allo Good-by. New York: E.P.
Dutton, 1940.
Account of a four-month trip through the United
States and Mexico with her husband.

831 Hutton, David Graham. Mexican Images. London:
Faber & Faber, 1963.

832   Huxley, Aldous Leonard. Beyond the Mexique Bay.
      London: Chatto & Windus, 1934; New York: Harper,
      1934.
           Account of a trip made by the English novelist and
           his wife through southern and central Mexico in
           1933. See also 235.

833   Iglehart, Fanny Chambers Gooch. Face to Face with
      the Mexicans: The Domestic Life, Educational, So-
      cial, and Business Ways ... as Seen and Studied by
      an American during Seven Years of Intercourse with
      Them. New York: Howard & Hulbert, 1887; London:
      S. Low, 1890.
           Memoirs by a Texan, who lived chiefly in Saltillo
           but also in Mexico City. See also 236.

834   Ingersoll, Ralph McAllister. In and under Mexico.
      London: T.W. Laurie, 1924; New York, London:
      Century, 1924.
           Memoirs of life in a copper mining camp, written
           by an American mining engineer.

      Ingram, David. See Hakluyt, R.

835   Jackson, Joseph Henry. Mexican Interlude. New York:
      Macmillan, 1936.
           Account of a trip made with his wife down the Pan-
           American highway to Mexico City and then out into
           the surrounding area. See also 239.

836   Jackson, Julia Newell. A Winter Holiday in Summer
      Lands. Chicago: A.C. McClurg, 1890.

837   Jacques, Mary J. Texan Ranch Life, with Three
      Months through Mexico in a "Prairie Schooner." Lon-
      don: 1894. [From Gardiner]

838   James, Neill. Dust on My Heart: Petticoat Vagabond
      in Mexico. New York: Scribner's, 1946.
           Memoir of four years of adventurous life.

839   James, Thomas. Three Years among the Indians and
      Mexicans, ed. Walter Bond Douglas. St. Louis:
      Missouri Historical Society, 1916.

840 Jamieson, Milton. Journal and Notes of a Campaign in
     Mexico ... with a Cursory Description of the Country,
     Climate, Cities, Waters, Roads, and Forts along the
     Southern Line of the American Army in Mexico; Also
     of the Manners and Customs, Agriculture, &c, of the
     Mexican People. Cincinnati: B. Franklin, 1849.

841 Jamieson, Tulitas Wulff (as told to Evelyn Jamieson
     Payne). Tulitas of Torreón: Reminiscences of Life
     in Mexico. El Paso: Texas Western, 1969.
     Memoir by the American wife of a mining engineer.

Janes, John F. See Hager, A. M.

842 Jebb, Bertha (Mrs. J. Gladwyn Jebb). A Strange
     Career: Life and Adventures of John Gladwyn Jebb.
     Edinburgh, London: W. Blackwood, 1894.
     Biography by his wife of an English mining engineer.
     See also 245.

843 Johnson, William Weber, and others. Mexico. London:
     Sunday Times, 1963; New York: Time, 1964.
     Description. The author has long been associated
     with the country.

Johnston, Abraham Robinson. See Bieber, R. P.

844 Johnstone, Nancy J. Sombreros Are Becoming. Lon-
     don: Faber & Faber, 1941; New York: Longmans,
     Green, 1941.
     Memoir about the eighteen months spent by the
     author and her husband in Cuernavaca.

845 Keiffer, Elisabeth. Year in the Sun. Indianapolis:
     Bobbs-Merrill, 1956.
     Memoir of a year spent with her family.

846 Keller, Weldon Philip. Travels of the Tortoise. Cran-
     bury, N.J.: A. S. Barnes, 1971; London: Jarrolds,
     1971.

847 Kendall, George Wilkins. Narrative of the Texas Santa
     Fé Expedition; Comprising a Description of a Tour
     through Texas and across the Great Southwestern
     Prairies, the Camanche and Caygüa Hunting-Grounds,
     with an Account of the Sufferings from Want of Food,

Losses from Hostile Indians, and Final Capture of the
Texans and Their March as Prisoners to the City of
Mexico. New York: Harper, 1844. Narrative of an
Expedition across the Great Southwestern Prairies
from Texas to Santa Fé.... London: D. Bogue,
1845.
Account by the New Orleans editor, who accom-
panied the 1841 expedition.

848 Kendall, John Jennings. Mexico under Maximilian.
London: Newby, 1871.

849 Kendall, John Smith. Seven Mexican Cities. New
Orleans: Picayune, 1906.

850 Kenly, John Reese. Memoirs of a Maryland Volunteer:
War with Mexico in the Years 1846-7-8. Philadelphia:
J. B. Lippincott, 1873.

851 Kennedy, Paul P. The Middle Beat: A Correspondent's
View of Mexico, Guatemala, and El Salvador, ed.
Stanley R. Ross. New York: Columbia University
Teachers College, 1971.
Memoir about the New York Times correspondent's
twelve years in these countries.

852 Ker, Henry. Travels through the Western Interior of
the United States from the Year 1808 up to the Year
1816, with a Particular Description of a Great Part
of Mexico, or New-Spain.... Elizabethtown, N. J.:
1816.

853 Ker, John L. Destination Topolobampo: The Kansas
City, Mexico, and Orient Railway. San Marino,
Calif.: 1968.

854 Kerouac, Jack (Jean Louis Lebris de Kerouac). Lone-
some Traveler. New York: McGraw-Hill, 1960;
London: A. Deutsch, 1962.
"Mexico Fellaheen": account of a trip from
Nogales to Mexico City to visit William Burroughs,
made in 1952. See also 253-257.

855 Kesey, Ken. Letters from Mexico. Armenian General
Benevolent Union, 1967.
Letters to Larry McMurtry from the American
novelist's flight from bail to Puerto Vallarta and
Manzanillo in 1966.

856 Kidd, Hari Matthew. Viva Mexico! Letters to V. J.
     Hooten, Editor, the El Paso Times. El Paso: 1943.

857 King, Rosa Eleanor. Tempest over Mexico: A Per-
     sonal Chronicle. Boston: Little, Brown, 1935; Lon-
     don: Methuen, 1936.
         Memoir of an Englishwoman's life in Cuernavaca,
     concentrating chiefly on the years between 1910
     and 1920.

858 Kingsley, Rose Georgina. South by West, or Winter
     in the Rocky Mountains and Spring in Mexico, ed.
     Charles Kingsley. London: W. Isbister, 1874.

859 Kirk, Betty. Covering the Mexican Front: The Battle
     of Europe versus America. Norman: University of
     Oklahoma, 1942.
         Interpretation of present-day conditions, made by
     an American journalist who spent six years in
     Mexico City.

860 Kirkham, Stanton Davis. Mexican Trails: A Record
     of Travel in Mexico, 1904-07, and a Glimpse at the
     Life of the Mexican Indian. New York, London:
     Putnam's, 1909.
         Memoirs of three years, including accounts of travel
     by horseback into little-visited places.

861 Kroupa, B. An Artist's Tour: Gleamings and Impres-
     sions of Travel in North and Central America and the
     Sandwich Islands. London: Ward & Downey, 1890.

862 Krutch, Joseph Wood. The Forgotten Peninsula: A
     Naturalist in Baja California. New York: W. Sloane,
     1961.
         Account of several visits made by the drama critic
     and naturalist.

863 La Farge, Oliver Hazard Perry. Raw Material. Bos-
     ton: Houghton Mifflin, 1945; London: V. Gollancz,
     1946.
         Memoirs, including a few comments on his archae-
     ological expedition into southern Mexico in 1925
     with Frans Blom.

864 Lamb, Dana, and June Cleveland. Enchanted Vagabonds.
     New York, London: Harper, 1938.

Account of a cruise made from San Diego to the
Panama Canal.

865 Lamb, Dana, and Virginia Bishop Lamb. Quest for
the Lost City. New York: Harper, 1951; London:
V. Gollancz, 1952.
Account of a trip through western Mexico to
Chiapas and a search there for an ancient Maya
city.

866 Lane, Walter P. The Adventures and Recollections of
General Walter P. Lane, a San Jacinto Veteran; Con-
taining Sketches of the Texian, Mexican, and Late
Wars. Marshall, Tex.: Tri-Weekly Herald, 1887.

867 Lanks, Herbert C. Nancy Goes to Mexico. Philadelphia: D. McKay, 1938.

_____. See also Franck, H. A.

868 Larkin, Margaret. Seven Shares in a Gold Mine. London: Gollancz, 1959; New York: Simon & Schuster,
1959.
Account by an American survivor of an airplane
explosion, deliberately set off, including the events
which led up to it and the trial afterwards.

869 Larkin, Thomas Oliver. First and Last Consul:
Thomas Oliver Larkin and the Americanization of
California; A Selection of Letters, ed. John Arkas
Hawgood. San Marino, Calif.: Huntington Library,
1962.

870 Larralde, Elsa. My House Is Yours. Philadelphia:
Lippincott, 1949.
Account about the troubles of building a house
near Cuernavaca.

871 Latrobe, Charles Joseph. The Rambler in Mexico,
MDCCCXXXIV. London: Seeley & Burnside, 1836;
México: Harper, 1836.

872 Lawrence, David Herbert. (a) The Letters..., ed.
Aldous Huxley. London: W. Heinemann, 1932; New
York: Viking, 1932. (b) Collected Letters, ed.
Harry Thornton Moore. London: Heinemann, 1962;
New York: Viking, 1962.

The English author made three visits to Mexico, with his wife and others, between 1923 and 1925, staying in Mexico City, Chapala, and Oaxaca. See also 267-269, 948.

873 _____. Mornings in Mexico. London: M. Secker, 1927; New York: Knopf, 1927.
"Corasmin and the Parrots," "Walk to Huayapa [sic]," "The Mozo," and "Market Days": accounts of the days before Christmas spent in Oaxaca in 1924.

874 Lawrenson, Helen. Latins Are Still Lousy Lovers. New York: Hawthorn, 1968.
"Mexicans Love Women" and "Nightmare of the Iguana" (essays): the second is about the filming of Tennessee Williams's play (534).

875 Leary, Timothy Francis. High Priest. New York: World, 1968.
Essays, including accounts of his drug experiences in various places in Mexico.

876 Lee, Allan W. The Burro and the Bibles, and Other Vignettes of a Summer in Mexico. New York: Exposition, 1968.

877 Lee, Jess. Smiling Huaraches: Magical Miles through Mexico. New York: Exposition, 1952.

878 Lee, (Mrs.) S.M. Glimpses of Mexico and California. Boston: G.H. Ellis, 1887.

Lee, William. See Burroughs, W.S.

879 Leigh, Randolph. Forgotten Waters: Adventures in the Gulf of California. Philadelphia: J.B. Lippincott, 1941.
Account of exploration in the Gulf in late 1940.

880 Lempriere, Charles. Notes in Mexico in 1861 and 1862, Politically and Socially Considered. London: Longman, Green, etc., 1862.

881 Leonard, Zenas. Narrative of the Adventures of Zenas Leonard, a Native of Clearfield County, Pa., Who Spent Five Years in Trapping for Furs, Trading with

the Indians ... of the Rocky Mountains. Clearfield,
Pa.: D. W. Moore, 1839.

882 Le Plongeon, Alice Dixon. Here and There in Yucatan:
Miscellanies. New York: J. W. Bouton, 1886.
See also 275.

883 Lilley, Peter, and Anthony Stansfeld (pseud. Dane
Chandos). House in the Sun. New York: Putnam's,
1949; London: M. Joseph, 1950.

884 Lilley, Peter, and Nigel Stansburg-Millet (pseud. Dane
Chandos). Village in the Sun. New York: Putnam's,
1945; London: M. Joseph, 1948.
Two memoirs [883-4] of life in Ajijic.

Lincoln, John. See Cardif, M.

885 Lindbergh, Anne Morrow. Bring Me a Unicorn: Diaries and Letters..., 1922-1928. New York: Harcourt, Brace, Jovanovich, 1972.
The American author was daughter of the ambas-
sador. (See also 941-942).

886 Linke, Lilo. Magic Yucatan: A Journey Remembered.
London: Hutchinson, 1950.

887 London, Charmian Kittredge. The Book of Jack London. New York: Century, 1921. Jack-London.
London: Mills & Boon, 1921.
Biography by his wife, including an account of
their trip to Veracruz in 1914 to cover the occupation.

888 Lorang, Mary Corde. Footloose Scientist in Mayan
America. New York: Scribner's, 1966.
Memoir of a year spent by the nun studying ar-
chaeological sites in Guatemala and Mexico.

889 Lowry, (Clarence) Malcolm. Selected Letters..., ed.
Harvey Breit and Margerie Bonner Lowry. Philadelphia: Lippincott, 1965; London: J. Cape, 1967.
Few letters from his first visit 1936-1938 and
more from his second in 1945-1946, as well as
comments about writing his Mexican novels. See
302-304. The author was English.

890 Lumholtz, Karl (or Carl) Sofus. New Trails in Mexico: An Account of One Year's Exploration in Northwestern Sonora, Mexico, and Southwestern Arizona, 1909-1910. London: T. F. Unwin, 1912; New York: Scribner's, 1912.

891 _____. Unknown Mexico: A Record of Five Years' Explorations among the Tribes of the Western Sierra Madre, in the Tierra Caliente of Tepic and Jalisco, and among the Tarascos of Michoachan. New York: Scribner's, 1902; London: Macmillan, 1903.

892 Lundy, Benjamin. The Life, Travels, and Opinions of Benjamin Lundy, Including His Journeys to Texas and Mexico, with a Sketch of Contemporary Events and a Notice of the Revolution in Hayti, ed. Thomas Earle. Philadelphia: W. D. Parrish, 1847.

893 Lydston, George Frank. Panama & the Sierras: A Doctor's Wander Days. Chicago: 1900. [From Gardiner]

894 Lyon, George Francis. Journal of a Residence and Tour in the Republic of Mexico in the Year 1826, with Some Account of the Mines of That Country. London: J. Murray, 1828.

895 _____. The Sketch-Book of Captain G. F. Lyon, R. N., during Eight Months Residence in Mexico. London: J. Dickinson, 1827.

896 McCall, George Archibald. Letters from the Frontiers, Written during a Period of Thirty Years' Service in the Army of the United States. Philadelphia: J. B. Lippincott, 1868.

897 McCarty, Fred M. Chihuahua al Pacifico: A Dream Come True. Amarillo, Tex.: 1968.

898 McCarty, Joseph Hendrickson. Two Thousand Miles through the Heart of Mexico. New York: Phillips & Hunt, 1886.

899 McClure, Alexander Kelly. To the Pacific & Mexico. Philadelphia: J. B. Lippincott, 1901.

900   McCollester, Sullivan Holman. Mexico Old and New,
       a Wonderland. 2nd ed. Boston: 1899. [From
       Gardiner]

901   McCoy, Alexander W., John McCoy, and Samuel Finley
       McCoy. Pioneering on the Plains; Journey to Mexico
       in 1848; The Overland Trip to California. Kankauna,
       Kan.: 1924.

902   McDonald, Marquis, and Glenn N. Oster. Baja: Land
       of Lost Missions. San Antonio: Naylor, 1968.

903   McElroy, Clarence L. Seventeen Days in the Mexican
       Jungle. Greenfield, Ind.: Mitchell, 1933.

904   McGary, Elizabeth Visère. An American Girl in Mexi-
       co. New York: Dodd, Mead, 1904.

905   M'Ilvaine, William Jr. Sketches of Scenery and Notes
       of Personal Adventure in California and Mexico.
       Philadelphia: Smith & Peters, 1850.

906   McNally. E. Evalyn Grumbine, and Andrew McNally.
       This Is Mexico. New York: Dodd, Mead, 1947.
       Interpretation of present conditions and history,
       written for teenagers. See also 315.

907   McNeil, Samuel. McNeil's Travels in 1849 to, through,
       and from the Gold Regions in California. Columbus,
       O.: Scott & Bascom, 1850.

908   McSherry, Richard. Essays and Lectures on: ... 2.
       Mexico and Mexican Affairs; 3. A Mexican Campaign
       ..., Baltimore: Kelly, Pict, 1869.

909   (and David Holmes Conrad). El Puchero, or
       A Mixed Dish from Mexico; Embracing General Scott's
       Campaign, with Sketches of Military Life in Field and
       Camp, of the Character of the Country, Manners and
       Ways of the People, etc. Philadelphia: Lippincott,
       Grumbo, 1850.

910   Magoffin, Susan Shelby. Down the Santa Fé Trail and
       into Mexico: The Diary of Susan Shelby Magoffin,
       1846-1847, ed. Stella M. Drumm. New Haven: Yale
       University, 1926.
       Notes written by an eighteen-year-old bride, who
       accompanied her husband to Santa Fe.

911 Magruder, Richard. Mexico: Moods and Images.
Dallas: Brodnax-Linn, 1962.

912 Mailer, Norman. The Bullfight: A Photographic Nar-
rative, with Text by Norman Mailer. New York:
Macmillan, 1967.
"Footnote to Death in the Afternoon" (essay): ob-
servations made in 1954 of novice bullfighters in
Mexico City.

913 Marett, Robert Hugh Kirk. An Eye-Witness of Mexico.
London: Oxford University Pr., 1939.

914 Martin, Percy Falcke. Mexico of the Twentieth Century.
London: E. Arnold, 1907.

915 Martin, Sylvia Pass. You Meet Them in Mexico. New
Brunswick, N.J.: Rutgers University, 1948.
Character studies based upon the people the author
knew while living in Cuernavaca or travelling
through the countryside.

916 Mason, Gregory. Silver Cities of Yucatan. New York;
London: G.P. Putnam's, 1927.
Account of a cruise by an archaeological team
searching out new sites along the coast. See also
327-328.

917 _____. South of Yesterday. New York: Holt,
1940.
Account of archaeological explorations in Yucatán
and in Columbia.

918 Mason, R.H. Pictures of Life in Mexico. London:
Smith, Elder, 1852.

919 Mathewson, Donna. Bananas Have No Bones. New
York: Comet, 1960.

920 _____. Down Mexico Way. New York: Comet,
1956.

921 Mathias, Fred S. The Amazing Bob Davis: His Last
Vagabond Journey. New York, Toronto: Longmans,
Green, 1944.
Account of a trip made by the American business-
man with the newspaper columnist, Robert Hobart
Davis, in 1941.

922 Maury, Dabney Herndon.   Recollections of a Virginian
     in the Mexican, Indian, and Civil Wars.   London:
     S. Low, 1894; New York: Scribner's, 1894.

923 Mayer, Brantz.   Mexico as It Was and as It Is.   New
     York: J. Winchester, 1844.

924 Merriam, Charles.   Machete: "It Happened in Mexico."
     Dallas: Southwest, 1932.
     Memoirs of an experience as amateur doctor by
     the young American, who had gone to work on his
     brother's sugar plantation on Tehuantepec.

925 Merritt-Hawkes, Onera Amelia.   High Up in Mexico.
     London: Nicholson & Watson, 1936.

926 Miles, Beryl.   Spirit of Mexico.   London: Murray,
     1961; New York: McBride, 1962.

927 Miles, William.   Journal of the Sufferings and Hard-
     ships of Capt. Parker H. French's Overland Expedi-
     tion to California, Which Left New York City, May
     13th, 1850, and Arrived at San Francisco, Dec. 14.
     Chambersburg, Pa.: Valley Spirit, 1851.

928 Miller, Max.   And Bring All Your Folk; Being a Light-
     hearted Examination of the Southern California Islands
     and Some Off Mexico, in Case We Get Crowded Off
     the Mainland!   Garden City: Doubleday, 1959.

929 _____.   The Cruise of the Cow; Being an Introduc-
     tion to San Diego, Mexico's Baja California, and a
     Voyage into the Gulf of California, This Combined
     Region of the Southwest Corner.   New York: Dutton,
     1951.
     Two accounts [928-9] of cruises by the San Diego
     journalist.

930 _____.   Land Where Time Stands Still.   New York:
     Dodd, Mead, 1943.
     Account of a trip down Baja California.

931 _____.   Mexico around Me.   London: Chatto &
     Windus, 1936; New York: Reynal & Hitchcock, 1937.
     Account of a trip to southern Mexico and Mexico
     City, with anecdotes about Emiliano Zapata.

932 Milliken, James. A Voyager's Letters from Mexico,
     1876. Philadelphia: 1876.

933 Mitchell-Hedges, Frederick Albert. Danger My Ally.
     London: Elek, 1954; Boston: Little, Brown, 1955.
     Autobiography of an Englishman who spent a check-
     ered career ranging from gambler to archaeologist.

934 Moats, Alice Leone. A Violent Innocence. New York:
     Duell, Sloan & Pearce, 1951.
     Memoirs of her childhood.

935 Moats, Leone Blakemore. Thunder in Their Veins:
     A Memoir of Mexico, ed. Russell Lord. New York,
     London: Century, 1932.
     Memoirs of more than twenty years in Mexico City
     by an American who went there as a young bride.

936 Moler, Arthur B. Mexico: The Diary of a Trip Taken
     by A. B. Moler and Wife, February 1912. Chicago:
     Legal News, 1928.

937 Moore, H. Judge. Scott's Campaign in Mexico from
     the Rendezvous on the Island of Lobos to the Taking
     of the City, including an Account of the Siege of
     Puebla, with Sketches of the Country and Manners
     and Customs of the Inhabitants. Charleston: J.B.
     Nixon, 1849.

938 Morris, Ann Axtell. Digging in Yucatan. Garden City:
     Doubleday, Doran, 1931.
     Memoirs of six years spent excavating Chichén
     Itzá, written for young people by the wife of the
     head archaeologist (see 939).

939 Morris, Earl Halstead. The Temple of the Warriors:
     The Adventure of Exploring and Restoring a Master-
     piece of Native American Architecture in the Ruined
     Maya City of Chichén Itzá, Yucatan. New York, Lon-
     don: Scribner's, 1931.
     Account of exploring and restoring a building.

940 Morris, Ida Dorman (Mrs. James Edwin Morris). A
     Tour in Mexico. New York: Abbey, 1902.

941 Morrow, Elizabeth Cutter. Casa Mañana. Croton
     Falls, N.Y.: Spiral, 1932.

The author was the wife of the American ambas-
sador. See also 342.

942 _____. The Mexican Years: Leaves from the Diary... New York: Spiral, 1953.

943 Moser, Edwa. The Mexican Touch. New York: Duell,
Sloane & Pearce, 1940.
Memoir of a year spent with her children in
Cuernavaca.

944 Murbarger, Nell. 30,000 Miles in Mexico: Adventures
of Two Women and a Pickup-Camper in Twenty-Eight
Mexican States. Palm Desert, Calif.: Desert Magazine, 1961.

945 Murphy, Charles J. Reminiscences of the War of the
Rebellion and of the Mexican War. New York: F.J.
Ficker, 1882.

946 Murray, Samuel. From Clime to Clime: Why and How
I Journeyed 21,630 Miles. New York: C.P. Young,
1905.

947 Murray, Spencer. Cruising the Sea of Cortez. Palm
Desert, Calif.: Desert-Southwest, 1963.
Account of exploration in the Gulf of California.

948 Nehls, Edward, ed. D.H. Lawrence: A Composite
Biography. Vol. 2. Madison: University of Wis-
consin, 1958.
Memoirs of life with the Lawrences in Mexico City,
Chapala, and Oaxaca, written by various people in-
cluding Dorothy Brett (619), Witter Bynner (638),
Kai Götzsche, Willard Johnson, Fred Leighton, and
Idella Purnell.

Nixon, Robert F. See Buck, R.

949 Norman, Benjamin Moore. Rambles by Land and Water,
or Notes of Travel in Cuba and Mexico, Including a
Canoe Voyage up the River Panuco and Researches
among the Ruins of Tamaulipas. New York: Paine
& Burgess, 1845.

950 _____. Rambles in Yucatan, or Notes of Travel
through the Peninsula, Including a Visit to the

Remarkable Ruins of Chi-Chen, Kabah, Zayi, and
Uxmal. New York: J. & H.C. Langley, 1843.

951 Northrop, Filmer Stuart Cuckow. The Meeting of East
     and West: An Inquiry Concerning World Understand-
     ing. New York: Macmillan, 1946.
        "The Rich Culture of Mexico" (essay): discussion
     of what Mexico has to offer to the spirit of the
     visitor from the United States or Great Britain.

952 Norton, Lewis Adelbut. Life and Adventures of Col.
     L.A. Norton, Written by Himself. Oakland: Pacific,
     1887.

953 Ober, Frederick Albion. Travels in Mexico and Life
     among the Mexicans. Boston: Estes & Lauriat,
     1884.
        See also 361.

954 O'Brien, Howard Vincent. Notes for a Book about Mexi-
     co. Chicago: Willet, Clark, 1937.
        Newspaper columns growing out of a two-month
     trip.

955 O'Brien, John Anthony. Discovering Mexico, a Country
     in Transition. Huntington, Ind.: Our Sunday Visitor,
     1943.

956 Olson, Charles. Mayan Letters, ed. Robert Creeley.
     Palma de Mallorca: Divers, 1954.
        The American poet and educator lived in Lerma,
     Campeche, with his wife 1950-1951.

957 Osbaldeston, Mitford W.B.J. Dawn Breaks in Mexico.
     London: Cassell, 1945.

958 Osbun, Albert Gallatin. To California and the South
     Seas: The Diary of Albert G. Osbun, 1849-1851, ed.
     John Haskell Kemble. San Marino, Calif.: Hunting-
     ton Library, 1966.

959 O'Shaughnessy, Edith Louise Coues. Diplomatic Days.
     New York: Harper, 1917.
        Letters to her mother by the wife of the American
     ambassador, covering the years 1911-1912.

960   . A Diplomat's Wife in Mexico: Letters from the American Embassy at Mexico City, Covering the Dramatic Period between October 8th, 1913, and the Breaking Off of Diplomatic Relations on April 23rd, 1914, Together with an Account of the Occupation of Vera Cruz. New York, London: Harper, 1916.

961   . Intimate Pages of Mexican History. New York: G. H. Doran, 1920.
Character studies of four presidents.

Oster, Glenn N. See McDonald, M.

962 Oswald, Felix Leopold. Summerland Sketches, or Rambles in the Backwoods of Mexico and Central America. Philadelphia: J. B. Lippincott, 1880.

963 Oswandel, J. Jacob. Notes of the Mexican War, 1846-47-48; Comprising Incidents, Adventures, and Every-day Proceedings, and Letters While with the United States Army in the Mexican War.... Rev. ed. Philadelphia: 1885.

964 Palmer, Frederick. Central America and Its Problems: An Account of a Journey from the Rio Grande to Panama, with Introductory Chapters on Mexico and Her Relations to Her Neighbors. London: T. W. Laurie, 1910; New York: Moffat, Yard, 1910.
Interpretation of present-day conditions.

965   . With My Own Eyes: A Personal Story of Battle Years. Indianapolis: Bobbs-Merrill, 1933; London: Jarrolds, 1934.
Memoir by the American journalist, including his experiences during the occupation of Veracruz in 1914.

966 Parker, Amos Andrew. Trip to the West and Texas; Comprising a Journey of Eight Thousand Miles through New York, Michigan, Illinois, Missouri, Louisiana, and Texas, in the Autumn and Winter of 1834-5; Interspersed with Anecdotes, Incidents, and Observations. Concord, N. H.: White & Fisher, 1836.

Parker, George. See Stoker, G. P.

967 Parmenter, Ross. Week in Yanhuitlán. Albuquerque:
     University of New Mexico, 1964.
     Account of the New York Times music editor's ex-
     ploration of a ruined monastery near Oaxaca.

968 Pattie, James Ohio. The Personal Narrative of James
     O. Pattie of Kentucky during an Expedition from St.
     Louis through the Vast Regions between That Place
     and the Pacific Ocean and Thence Back through the
     City of Mexico to Vera Cruz, during Journeyings of
     Six Years..., ed. Timothy Flint. Cincinnati: E. H.
     Flint, 1833.

969 Payne, Etta. Land-Yachting to Central America: A
     Trailer's-Eye View of Our Nearest Latin Neighbors.
     New York: Greenwich Book, 1960.

970 Peck, John James. The Sign of the Eagle: A View of
     Mexico, 1830-1855; Letters of Lt. John James Peck,
     U.S. Soldier in the Mexican War..., ed. Richard F.
     Pourade. San Diego: Union-Tribune, 1970.

971 Peissel, Michel. The Lost World of Quintana Roo.
     New York: Dutton, 1963; London: Hodder & Stough-
     ton, 1964.
          Chronicle of two journeys, the first a walking tour
     along the coast in 1958. The French-born author
     was educated in the United States.

972 Pellowe, William Charles Smithson. The Royal Road
     to Mexico: A Travel Log--An Interpretation--A Plea
     for Friendship. Detroit: Watergate, 1937.

973 Pendergast, David M., ed. Palenque: The Walker-
     Caddy Expedition to the Ancient Maya City, 1839-
     1840. Norman: University of Oklahoma, 1967.
          Diary and report of the expedition made by the two
     Englishmen from Belize to Palenque.

974 Philips, John. An Authentic Journal of the Late Expe-
     dition under the Command of Commodore Anson.
     London: J. Robinson, 1744.
          Account of a voyage around the world which touched
     briefly the Pacific coast of Mexico.

     Philips, Miles. See Hakluyt, R.

975 Phillips, John. Mexico Illustrated.... London: E.
     Atchley, 1848.

976 Pike, Zebulon Montgomery. (a) An Account of Expedi-
     tions ... and a Tour through the Interior Parts of
     New Spain When Conducted through These Provinces
     by Order of the Captain-General in the Year 1807.
     Philadelphia: C. & A. Conrad, 1810. (b) Exploratory
     Travels ... and a Journey through Louisiana and the
     North Eastern Provinces of New Spain, Performed in
     the Years 1805, 1806, 1807, ed. T. Rees. London:
     Longman, 1811. (c) The Journals..., with Letters
     and Related Documents, ed. Donald Jackson. Norman:
     University of Oklahoma, 1966.
     The American explorer was captured near Santa
     Fe and marched to Chihuahua before being released.

     Pinchon, Edgcumb. See Gutiérrez de Lara, L.

977 Pitkin, Winifred. Hidden Cities of Middle America:
     The Archaeological Adventures of a Septuagenarian.
     Glasgow: W. MacLellan, 1959.

978 Pleasants, Joseph Edward. The Cattle Drives of Joseph
     E. Pleasants from Baja California in 1867 and 1868,
     ed. Don Meadows. Los Angeles: Dawson's Book
     Shop, 1965.

979 Poinsett, Joel Roberts. Notes on Mexico Made in the
     Autumn of 1822...; by a Citizen of the United States.
     Philadelphia: Carey & Lea, 1824; London: J. Miller,
     1825.
     Account of a fact-finding expedition made through
     northern and central Mexico by the future first
     American minister.

980 Pollard, Hugh Bertie Campbell. A Busy Time in Mexi-
     co: An Unconventional Record of Mexican Incident.
     London: Constable, 1913; New York: Duffield, 1913.
     Memoirs and interpretation of the present situation
     by a journalist.

981 Poole, Annie Sampson. Mexicans at Home in the In-
     terior; by a Resident. London: Chapman & Hall,
     1884.

982 Porter, James A. Doctor, Spare My Cow! Ames:
     Iowa State College, 1956.

Account of the campaign against hoof-and-mouth
disease.

983 Porter, Katherine Anne. (a) The Days Before. New
York: Harcourt, Brace, 1952; London: Secker &
Warburg, 1953. (b) The Collected Essays and Occa-
sional Writings. New York: Delacorte, 1970.
(a-b) "Why I Write about Mexico," "Leaving the
Petate," "The Mexican Trinity," "La Conquista-
dora," "Quetzalcoatl," "The Charmed Life"; (b)
"St. Augustine and the Bullfight," "The Fiesta of
Guadalupe," and "Where Presidents Have No
Friends" (essays and reviews). Also "Two Songs
from Mexico" (poems). The American author
visited Mexico in her childhood and lived in Mexico City off and on from 1920 until 1931. See also
378-379.

984 Portlock, Nathaniel. A Voyage round the World, but
More Particularly to the North-West Coast of Amer-
ica, Performed in 1785, 1786, 1787, and 1788....
London: Stockdale & Goulding, 1789.

985 Prentis, Noble Lovely. South-Western Letters. Topeka:
Kansas, 1882.

986 Preston, William. Journal in Mexico, Dating from
November 1, 1847, to May 25, 1848. Paris: n.d.

987 Preuss, Charles. Exploring with Frémont: The Pri-
vate Diaries of Charles Preuss, Cartographer for
John C. Frémont on His First, Second, and Fourth
Expeditions to the Far West, ed. Erwin G. and
Elisabeth K. Gudde. Norman: University of Oklaho-
ma, 1958.
Diaries of the German-American, translated from
the German, about his exploration of California.

988 Price, Rose Lambert. The Two Americas: An Ac-
count of Sport and Travel, with Notes on Men and
Manners in North and South America. London: Low,
Marston, etc., 1877; Philadelphia: Lippincott, 1877.
Account of a trip made by the British nobleman.

989 Price, Thomas W. Brief Notes Taken on a Trip to
the City of Mexico in 1878. N.p.: n.d.

990 Price, Willard. Roving South: Rio Grande to Patagonia.
     New York: J. Day, 1948. Tropic Adventure: Rio
     Grande to Patagonia. London: Heinemann, 1949.
     Account of a trip made with his wife from Mexico
     through South America.

991 Pringle, Cyrus Guernsey. Life and Work..., ed.
     Helen Burns Davis. Burlington, Vt.: Free Press,
     1936.
     "Diaries of Mexican Trips" and "Notes on Mexican
     Travel."

992 Prouty, Amy. Mexico and I. Philadelphia: Dorrance,
     1951.
     Account of a visit.

993 Purcell, William Louis. Frontier Mexico, 1875-1894:
     Letters, ed. Anita Purcell. San Antonio: Naylor,
     1963.

994 Purdie, Samuel A. Memories of Angela Aguilar de
     Mascorro and Sketches of the Friends' Mexican Mis-
     sion. Chicago: 1885. [From Gardiner]

995 Puxley, W. Lavillin. The Magic Land of the Maya.
     London: Allen & Unwin, 1928.

996 Ramsey, Leonidas Willing. Time Out for Adventure:
     Let's Go to Mexico. Garden City: Doubleday, Doran,
     1934; London: S. Paul, 1934.
     Account of a trip made by an advertising man and
     an artist.

997 Record, Paul. Tropical Frontier. New York: Knopf,
     1969.
     Memoir about over two years spent farming in
     southeastern Mexico.

998 Reed, John (Silas). Insurgent Mexico. New York,
     London: D. Appleton, 1914.
     Account of his experiences in the Mexican Revolu-
     tion 1913-1914, chiefly spent with Francisco Villa.
     See also 391.

999 Rees, Thomas. Spain's Lost Jewels: Cuba and Mexi-
     co. Springfield: Illinois State Register, 1906.

Reid, Thomas Mayne. See 392-397, 1149.

1000 Remington, Frederic. Pony Tracks. New York:
Harper, 1895.
"An Outpost of Civilization," "A Rodeo at Los
Ojos," "In the Sierra Madre with the Punchers,"
and "Coaching in Chihuahua" (essays with illustrations): accounts of exploration in northern Mexico by the American painter.

1001 Rice, John H. Mexico, Our Neighbor. New York:
J. W. Lovell, 1888.

1002 Richard, Thomas Arthur. Journeys of Observation.
San Francisco: Dewey, 1907.
"Among the Mines of Mexico": account of a trip
made by the American mining engineer.

Ricketts, Edward F. See Steinbeck, J.

1003 Ripley, Eliza Moore McHatton. From Flag to Flag:
A Woman's Adventures and Experiences in the South
during the War, in Mexico, and in Cuba. New York:
D. Appleton, 1889.

1004 Roberts, Edwards. With the Invader: Glimpses of
the Southwest. San Francisco: S. Carson, 1885.

1005 Robertson, John Blount. Reminiscences of a Campaign
in Mexico; by a Member of "The Bloody-First."
Nashville: J. York, 1849.

1006 Robertson, William Parish. A Visit to Mexico by the
West India Islands, Yucatan, and United States, with
Observations and Adventures on the Way. London:
Simpkin, Marshall, 1853.

1007 Robinson, Alfred. Life in California during a Residence of Several Years in That Territory; Comprising a Description of the Country and the Missionary
Establishments, with Incidents, Observations, etc.;
by an American. New York: Wiley & Putnam,
1846.

1008 Robinson, Jacob S. Sketches of the Great West: A
Journal of the Santa-Fe Expedition under Col.
Doniphan, Which Left St. Louis in June 1846.

Portsmouth, N. H.: Portsmouth Journal, 1848.

1009 Robinson, William Davis. Memoirs of the Mexican
      Revolution, including a Narrative of the Expedition
      of General Xavier Mina. ... Philadelphia: L. R.
      Bailey, 1820; London: 1821.
        The American author saw part of the War for
        Independence.

1010 Rodenbough, Theophilus Francis, ed. From Everglade
      to Cañon with the Second Dragoons (Second United
      States Cavalry): An Authentic Account of Service in
      Florida, Mexico, Virginia, and the Indian Country...,
      1836-1875. New York: Van Nostrand, 1875.

1011 Rodman, Selden. Mexican Journal: The Conquerors
      Conquered; A Journal of Six Months in Mexico, In-
      cluding Travel to the Principal Parts of That Coun-
      try, Conversations with Distinguished Personalities
      in the Arts and Public Life, Adventures, Mishaps,
      Reflections, and Photographs. New York: Devin-
      Adair, 1958.
        Account of a trip made by the American poet in
        1956-1957, primarily in central and southern
        Mexico.

1012 _____. The Road to Panama. New York: Haw-
      thorn, 1966.
        Opening chapters concern Mexico. Some of the
        material appeared in 1011.

1013 Rogers, Thomas L. Mexico? Si, Señor. Boston:
      1893.

1014 Rogers, Woodes. A Cruising Voyage round the World,
      First to the South-Seas, Thence to the East-Indies,
      and Homewards by the Cape of Good Hope, Begun in
      1708 and Finish'd in 1711. ... London: Bell &
      Lintot, 1712.

1015 Rosa, Guido. Mexico Speaks. New York: J. Day,
      1944.
        Account of a trip.

1016 Royer, Fanchón. The México We Found. Milwaukee:
      Bruce, 1948.

Account of a visit made with her daughters while the author was directing educational films.

1017 Russell, Phillips. Red Tiger: Adventures in Yucatan and Mexico. London: Hodder & Stoughton, 1929; New York: Brentano's, 1929. Account of a trip through southern Mexico made with an artist friend.

Rutgers, Lispenard. See Smith, H. E.

1018 Ruxton, George Frederick Augustus. Adventures in Mexico and the Rocky Mountains. London: J. Murray, 1847; New York: Harper, 1848. Account of a trip made by the British adventurer during the Mexican-American War.

1019 Ryan, William Redmond. Personal Adventures in Upper and Lower California in 1848-9, with the Author's Experiences at the Mines. London: W. Shoberl, 1850.

1020 Safley, James Clifford. Mexican Vistas. San Diego: Union-Tribune, 1952.

1021 Sanborn, Helen Josephine. A Winter in Central America and Mexico. Boston: Lee & Shepard, 1886.

1022 Sanford, Jeremy. In Search of the Magic Mushroom: A Journey through Mexico. London: P. Owen, 1972.

1023 Sanford, Paul. Where the Old West Never Died. San Antonio: Naylor, 1968.

1024 Schaeffer, Luther Melanchthon. Sketches of Travel in South America, Mexico, and California. New York: J. Egbert, 1860.

1025 Schell, Rolfe F. Yank in Yucatan: Adventures and Guide through Eastern Mexico. Fort Meyers Beach, Fla.: Islands, 1963.

1026 Schroeder, Seaton. The Fall of Maximilian's Empire as Seen from a United States Gun-Boat. New York: G. P. Putnam's, 1887.

1027 Schwatka, Frederick. In the Land of Cave and Cliff
      Dwellers. New York: Cassell, 1893.

1028 Scribner, Benjamin Franklin. Camp Life of a Volun-
      teer: A Campaign in Mexico, or a Glimpse of Life
      in Camp; by "One Who Has Seen the Elephant."
      Philadelphia: Grigg, Elliot, 1847.
      Memoir of experiences in the Mexican-American
      War.

1029 Seeburger, Merze Marvin. Gringoes across the Bor-
      der. New York: Pageant, 1954.

1030 Semmes, Raphael. Service Afloat and Ashore during
      the Mexican War. Cincinnati: W.H. Moore, 1851.

1031 Shaffer, Zepherine Towne. I Went to Mexico: A Nar-
      rative of the Good Will Tour of the Daughters of the
      Revolution Party to Mexico, Jl. 19-Aug. 11, 1941;
      Glimpses of the Mystery of the Montezumas; A
      Charming and Progressive Land with a Wonderful
      Future. Otsego, Mich.: Otsego Union, 1941.

1032 Shaler, William. Journal of a Voyage between China
      and the Northwestern Coast of America Made in
      1804. Philadelphia: 1808.

1033 Shelvocke, George. A Voyage round the World by Way
      of the Great South Sea, Perform'd in the Years 1719,
      20, 21, 22, in the Speedwell of London.... London:
      J. Senex, 1726.

1034 Shepard, Ashbel K. The Land of the Aztecs, or Two
      Years in Mexico. Albany: Weed, Parsons, 1859.

1035 Shepherd, Grant. The Silver Magnet: Fifty Years in
      a Mexican Silver Mine. New York: E.P. Dutton,
      1938.
      Memoirs of family life in a Chihuahua mining
      area, beginning in 1880.

1036 Sheridan, Clare Consuelo Frewen. My American
      Diary. New York: Boni & Liveright, 1922.
      Account of a trip made by the artist to the United
      States and Mexico.

1037 Sherratt, Harriott Wight. Mexican Vistas Seen from High-

ways and By-Ways of Travel. Chicago: Rand, Mc-
Nally, 1899.

1038 Shields, Karena. The Changing Wind. New York:
Crowell, 1959; London: J. Murray, 1960.
Memoirs of her childhood on a rubber plantation
in southern Mexico.

1039 Shoemaker, Michael Myers. The Kingdom of the
"White Woman": A Sketch. Cincinnati: R. Clarke,
1894.

1040 Simpson, George. Narrative of a Journey round the
World during the Years 1841 and 1842. London:
H. Colburn, 1847. An Overland Journey round the
World during the Years 1841 and 1842. Philadelphia:
Lea & Blanchard, 1847.

1041 Sitwell, Sacheverell. Golden Wall and Mirador: From
England to Peru. London: Weidenfeld & Nicolson,
1961. Golden Wall and Mirador: Travels and Observations in Peru. Cleveland: World, 1961.
Account of a trip made by the English poet and
essayist, including a visit to Yucatán in 1960.

1042 _____. Journey to the Ends of Time. Vol. 1:
Lost in the Dark Wood. London: Cassell, 1959;
New York: Random House, 1959.
Essay, sometimes colored by the author's 1952
trip.

1043 Skeaping, John Rattenbury. The Big Tree of Mexico.
London: Turnstile, 1952; Bloomington: Indiana University, 1953.

1044 A Sketch of the Customs and Society of Mexico in a
Series of Familiar Letters, and a Journal of Travels
in the Interior during the Years 1824, 1825, 1826.
London: Longman, 1828.

1045 Sketches of the War in Northern Mexico, with Pictures
of Life, Manners, and Scenery. New York: D.
Appleton, 1848.

1046 Smart, Charles Allen. At Home in Mexico. Garden
City: Doubleday, 1957.

Memoirs of several years spent by the author
and his wife in San Miguel de Allende.

1047 Smith, Ann Eliza Brainerd (Mrs. J. Gregory Smith).
      Notes of Travel in Mexico and California. St.
      Albans, Vt.: Messanger & Advertiser, 1886.

1048 Smith, Ephraim Kirby. To Mexico with Scott: Letters
      of Captain E. Kirby Smith to His Wife, ed. Emma
      Jerome Blackwood. Cambridge: Harvard University,
      1917.

1049 Smith, Francis Hopkinson. A White Umbrella in Mexi-
      co. Boston: Houghton Mifflin, 1889; London: Long-
      mans, 1889.

1050 Smith, George Winston, and Charles Judah, eds.
      Chronicles of the Gringos: The U.S. Army in the
      Mexican War, 1846-1848; Accounts of Eyewitnesses
      & Combatants. Albuquerque: University of New
      Mexico, 1968.

1051 Smith, Harry Allen. The Pig in the Barber Shop.
      Boston: Little, Brown, 1958.
        Account of a trip made by the American humorist.

1052 Smith, Henry Erskine (pseud. Lispenard Rutgers). On
      and Off the Saddle: Characteristic Sights and Scenes
      from the Great Northwest to the Antilles. New York:
      G. P. Putnam's, 1894.

1053 Smith, Isaac. Reminiscences of a Campaign in Mexi-
      co: An Account of the Operations of the Indiana
      Brigade on the Line of the Rio Grande and Sierra
      Madres.... Indianapolis: Chapmans & Spann, 1848.

      Smith, Walter Gifford. See Hager, A. M.

1054 Spratling, William Philip. File on Spratling: An
      Autobiography. Boston: Little, Brown, 1967.
        Memoirs, concentrating chiefly on the American
      silversmith's years in Taxco 1929-1967.

1055 _____. Little Mexico. New York: Cape & Smith,
      1932.
        Later called A Small Mexican World. Descrip-
      tion of Taxco and environs.

1056 Spring, Arthur L. Beyond the Rio Grande: A Jour-
      ney in Mexico. Boston: J. S. Adams, 1886.

1057 Squier, Emma Lindsay. Gringa: An American Wom-
      an in Mexico. Boston: Houghton Mifflin, 1934.
      Account of two trips, the first a cruise along the
      west coast and a stay in Guadalajara, the second
      a visit with her husband to Mexico City and
      southern Mexico. See also 452.

1058 Stacy-Judd, Robert Benjamin. Kabah: Adventures in
      the Jungles of Yucatan. Hollywood: House-Warren,
      1951.

      Stansburg-Millet, Nigel. See Lilley, P.

      Stansfeld, Anthony. See Lilley, P.

1059 Stapp, William Preston. The Prisoners of Perote;
      Containing a Journal Kept by the Author, Who Was
      Captured by the Mexicans at Mier, December 25,
      1842, and Released from Perote, May 16, 1844.
      Philadelphia: G. B. Zieber, 1845.

1060 Starr, Frederick. In Indian Mexico: A Narrative of
      Travel and Labor. Chicago: Forbes, 1908.
      Account of the American ethnologist's trip through
      Indian communities of central and southern Mexi-
      co.

1061 Steele, James. Old Californian Days. Chicago: Bel-
      ford-Clarke, 1889.

1062 Steffens, Joseph Lincoln. The Autobiography of Lin-
      coln Steffens. London: G. G. Harrap, 1931; New
      York: Harcourt, Brace, 1931.
      The American writer made three trips to Revolu-
      tionary Mexico--in 1914, 1915-1916, and 1921--
      and worked for the Revolutionists' cause in the
      United States.

1063 _____. The Letters of Lincoln Steffens, ed. Ella
      Winter and Granville Hicks. New York: Harcourt,
      Brace, 1938.

1064 _____. The World of Lincoln Steffens, ed. Ella
      Winter and Herbert Shapiro. New York: Hill &
      Wang, 1962.

"The Sunny Side of Mexico" and "Making Friends with Mexico" (essays).

1065   Steinbeck, John (with Edward F. Ricketts). Sea of Cortez: A Leisurely Journal of Travel and Research.... New York: Viking, 1941. First part reissued under Steinbeck's name alone as The Log from the Sea of Cortez. Account of an expedition to the Gulf of California in 1940. See also 455-456.

1066   Stephens, John Lloyd. Incidents of Travel in Central America, Chiapas, and Yucatan. London: J. Murray, 1841; New York: Harper, 1841. Account of an expedition by the American author, in company with Frederick Catherwood, to search out Maya ruins. This book set forth the first news that this civilization had ever existed.

1067   _____. Incidents of Travel in Yucatan. London: 1843; New York: Harper, 1843. Account of the pair's return 1841-1842 for further exploration.

1068   Stephens, Roger. Down That Pan American Highway. New York: 1948.

1069   Stevenson, Sara Yorke. Maximilian in Mexico: A Woman's Reminiscences of the French Intervention, 1862-1867. New York: Century, 1899.

1070   Stewart, George Rippey. N.A.1: The North-South Continental Highway. Boston: Houghton Mifflin, 1957. Description of the highway north to Alaska and south to Costa Rica.

1071   Stoker, Catharine Ulmer. Under Mexican Skies. Dallas: Upshaw, 1947. See also 458.

1072   Stoker, George Parker (pseud. Dr. George Parker). Guarache Trail: Adventures of an American Doctor Battling for a "Lost" Silver Mine in the Bandit Country of Northern Mexico. New York: Dutton, 1951.

Memoirs of some ten years at the beginning of the century, first as doctor on the oil fields and then in the Revolution.

1073 Stoner, Elsie Shaw, and Allen Stoner. Vacation Daze: Our Mexican Marriage and Other Travel Adventures. Raleigh: Capitol College, 1957.

1074 Stoppelman, Joseph Willem Ferdinand. People of Mexico. London: Phoenix House, 1964; New York: Hastings House, 1966.
Character studies, mostly of Indians, made by the journalist, who lived for more than a year in Mexico City.

1075 _____. Zo Is Mexico. Amsterdam: Broekman & DeMeris, 1963.

1076 Storm, Marian. Hoofways into Hot Country. México: Bland, 1939.
See also 460-461.

1077 _____. Prologue to Mexico: The Story of a Search for a Place. New York: 1931. Little-Known Mexico: The Story of a Search for a Place. London: Hutchinson, 1932.
Account of travel seeking out a place to live, finally realized in Uruapan.

1078 Street, George G. Che! Wah! Wah! or The Modern Montezumas in Mexico. Rochester: E. R. Andrews, 1883.

1079 Strode, Hudson. Now in Mexico. New York: Harcourt, Brace, 1947.
Description, based on ten years of travel.

Sullivan, Margaret Frances Buchanan. See Blake, M. E.

1080 Swan, Michael. Temples of the Sun and Moon: A Mexican Journey. London: J. Cape, 1954.

1081 Tayloe, Edward Thornton. Mexico, 1825-1828: The Journals and Correspondence..., ed. Clinton Harvey

Gardiner. Chapel Hill: University of North Carolina, 1959.
> Notes made by the secretary of the first American
> minister to Mexico, Joel R. Poinsett.

1082 Taylor, Bayard. Eldorado, or Adventures in the Path
of Empire; Comprising a Voyage to California via
Panama, Life in San Francisco and Monterey, Pictures of the Gold Region, and Experiences of Mexican Travel. London: R. Bentley, 1850; New York:
G. P. Putnam, 1850.
> Account of a journey made by the American poet
> from Mazatlán to Veracruz 1849-1850.

1083 Taylor, Fitch Waterman. The Broad Pennant, or A
Cruise in the United States Flag Ship of the Gulf
Squadron during the Mexican Difficulties, Together
with Sketches of the Mexican War from the Com-
mencement of Hostilities to the Capture of the City
of Mexico. New York: Leavitt, Trow, 1848.

1084 Tennery, Thomas D. The Mexican War Diary..., ed.
D. E. Livingston-Little. Norman: University of
Oklahoma, 1971.

1085 Terrell, Alexander Watkins. From Texas to Mexico
and the Court of Maximilian in 1865. Dallas: Book
Club of Texas, 1933.

1086 Thomas, Lowell Jackson (with Rex Barton). Seeing
Mexico with Lowell Thomas. Akron, O., New York:
Saalfield, 1937.

1087 Thomas, Pascoe. A True and Impartial Journal of
a Voyage to the South-Seas and round the Globe in
His Majesty's Ship the Centurion under the Command
of Commodore George Anson.... London: S. Birt,
1745.

1088 Thomas, Peggy Iris. Gasoline Gypsy. New York:
Crowell, 1953. A Ride in the Sun. London: Hodder & Stoughton, 1954.
> Account by an English schoolteacher of her trip
> through Canada, the United States, and Mexico.

1089 Thomas, Robert Horatio, ed. Journalists' Letters
Descriptive of Texas and Mexico. Mechanicsburg,
Pa.: 1889. [From Gardiner]

1090   Thompson, Edward Herbert.   People of the Serpent:
       Life and Adventures among the Mayas.   Boston:
       Houghton Mifflin, 1932; London: G. P. Putnam's,
       1933.
           Memoirs of twenty years in Yucatán as American
           consul and as archaeologist.   See also 478.

1091   Thompson, George Alexander.   Narrative of an Offi-
       cial Visit to Guatemala from Mexico.   London: J.
       Murray, 1829.

1092   Thompson, John Eric Stanley.   Maya Archaeologist.
       London: R. Hale, 1963; Norman: University of
       Oklahoma, 1963.
           Memoir of the years spent by the English ar-
           chaeologist on expeditions in Mexico and Central
           America.

1093   Thompson, Nora Belle.   Vignettes from South of the
       Border.   Kutztown, Pa.:   Kutztown, 1940.

1094   Thompson, Waddy.   Recollections of Mexico.   New
       York: Wiley & Putnam, 1846.
           Memoir by the American minister 1842-1844.

1095   Thomson, W. H.   Personal Impressions of a Trip to
       the City of Mexico and through California on the
       Good Car Lycoming.   N. p.:   1884. [From Gardiner]

1096   Tilden, Bryant Parrot.   Notes on the Upper Rio
       Grande ... Explored in the Months of October and
       November 1846 on Board the U. S. Steamer Major
       Brown, Commanded by Capt. Mark Sterling of
       Pittsburg....   Philadelphia: Lindsay & Blakiston,
       1847.

1097   Timberman, O. W.   Mexico's "Diamond in the Rough":
       Lower California Adventure.   Los Angeles: Western-
       lore, 1959.

       Tomson, Robert.   See Hakluyt, R.

       Torsvan, Traven.   See Traven, B.

1098   Travels of Anna Bishop in Mexico, 1849.   Philadelphia:
       C. Deal, 1852.

1099   Traven, B. (Traven Torsvan). Land des Frühlings.
       Berlin: Büchergilde Gutenberg, 1928.
       Description of Chiapas, with photographs made
       by the American writer. See 484-496.

1100   Travis, William Barret. Diary, August 30, 1833 -
       June 26, 1834, ed. Robert E. Davis. Trans.
       Thomas W. Walker. Waco: Texian, 1966.
       Account by an early settler of Texas.

1101   Trend, John Brande. Mexico: A New Spain with Old
       Friends. Cambridge: Cambridge University, 1940;
       New York: Macmillan, 1941.
       Account of two visits, one of sixteen days in 1938
       and the other of six months in 1939, made by a
       Cambridge University professor of Spanish.

1102   Treviño, Elizabeth Borton. My Heart Lies South:
       The Story of My Mexican Marriage. New York:
       Crowell, 1953; London: V. Gollancz, 1954.
       Memoir of the American journalist's marriage to
       a businessman in Monterrey. See also 498-503.

1103   _____. Where the Heart Is. Garden City: Double-
       day, 1962.

1104   Trueheart, James L. The Perote Prisoners; Being the
       Diary of James L. Trueheart..., ed. Frederick
       Charles Chabot. San Antonio: Naylor, 1934.
       Account of an incident in the Texas fight.

1105   Tschiffely, Aimé Felix. Southern Cross to Pole Star.
       London: Heinemann, 1933. Tschiffely's Ride: Ten
       Thousand Miles in the Saddle from Southern Cross
       to Pole Star. New York: Simon & Schuster, 1933.
       Account of a horseback ride from Buenos Aires
       to Washington, D.C., taking two-and-a-half years.

1106   Tudor, Henry. Narrative of a Tour in North America,
       comprising Mexico, the Mines of Real del Monte,
       the United States, and British Colonies, with an Ex-
       cursion to Cuba, in a Series of Letters Written in
       the Years 1831-2. London: J. Duncan, 1834.

1107   Turner, Henry Smith. The Original Journals of

Henry Smith Turner with Stephen Watts Kearny to
New Mexico and California, 1846-1847, ed. Dwight
Lancelot Clarke. Norman: University of Oklahoma,
1966.

1108 Turner, John Kenneth. Barbarous Mexico. Chicago:
      C.H. Kern, 1911. Barbarous Mexico: An Indict-
      ment of a Cruel and Corrupt System. London: Cas-
      sell, 1911.
         Interpretation of present conditions, sympathetic
      completely to the Revolutionists' side.

1109 Turner, Timothy Gilman. Bullets, Bottles, and
      Gardenias. Dallas: South-West, 1935.

1110 Tweedie, Ethel Brilliana Harley (Mrs. Alec Tweedie).
      Mexico as I Saw It. London: Hurst & Blackett,
      1901.

      Tyler, Marian. See Chase, S.

1111 Tylor, Edward Burnett. Anahuac, or Mexico and the
      Mexicans, Ancient and Modern. London: Longman,
      Green, etc., 1861.

1112 Vancouver, George. A Voyage of Discovery to the
      Pacific Ocean and round the World, in Which the
      Coast of North-West America Has Been Carefully
      Examined and Accurately Surveyed ... Performed
      in the Years 1790, 1791, 1792, 1793, 1794, and
      1795... London: G.G. & J. Robinson, 1798.
         The English expedition explored the coastline of
      California.

1113 Van Sinderen, Adrian. A Journey into Neolithic Times.
      New York: 1947.

1114 Vigne, Godfrey Thomas. Travels in Mexico, South
      America, etc. London: W.H. Allen, 1863.

1115 Vinding, Diana. Mexico. London: Methuen, 1968.

1116 A Visit to Texas; Being the Journal of a Traveller
      through Those Parts Most Interesting to American
      Settlers.... New York: Goodrich & Wiley, 1834.

Walker, Patrick.   See Pendergast, D. M.

1117   Wallace, Dillon.   Beyond the Mexican Sierra.   Chicago:
       A.C. McClurg, 1910; London: Hodder & Stoughton,
       1910.

1118   Wallace, Lewis.   Lew Wallace: An Autobiography.
       New York, London: Harper, 1906.
               Incomplete memoirs.   The American writer was
       in the Mexican-American War and returned later
       several times in an effort to help Benito Juárez
       against Maximilian.   See also 512.

1119   Wallace, Lucy H.   The Incredible City: Real de
       Catorce, Mexico.   Mission, Tex.:   Amigo Enter-
       prises, 1965.
               Description of a hidden town in northern Mexico.

1120   Walter, Richard, ed.   A Voyage round the World in
       the Years MDCCXL, I, II, III, IV; by George Anson.
       London: J. & P. Knapton, 1748.

1121   Ward, Henry George.   Mexico in 1827.   London: H.
       Colburn, 1828.
               Account of travel and description of the country
       by the English charge d'affairs 1825-1827.

1122   Warner, Charles Dudley.   On Horseback--A Tour in
       Virginia, North Carolina, and Tennessee; With
       Notes of Travel in Mexico and California.   Boston:
       Houghton Mifflin, 1888.
               Account of a rail trip made by the American
       writer and editor in 1887 to Mexico City.

1123   Warner, Louis Henry.   Mexico's Progress Demands
       Its Price.   Boston: Chapman & Grimes, 1937.
               Account of a trip and interpretation of present
       conditions.

1124   Waters, Frank.   Pumpkin Seed Point.   Chicago: Sage
       Books, 1969.
               Memoirs of life among the Indians of northern
       Mexico and Arizona.   See also 513-514.

1125   Watson, Jane Coulson.   South to Mexico.   New York:
       H. Holt, 1939.

1126 Waugh, Evelyn. Robbery under Law: The Mexican
      Object-Lesson. London: Chapman & Hall, 1939.
      Mexico: An Object Lesson. Boston: Little, Brown,
      1939.
          Interpretation of present conditions, based upon a
          visit made by the English novelist in 1938.

1127 Webb, James Josiah. Adventures in the Santa Fé
      Trade, 1844-1847, ed. Ralph Paul Bieber. Glendale,
      Calif.: A.H. Clark, 1931.

1128 Weeks, George F. California Copy. Washington:
      Washington College, 1928.
          Memoir, including account of journalism in Mexi-
          co City.

1129 _____ (pseud. "El Gringo"). Mexico from Muleback:
      In the Footprints of the Spanish Pioneers. New York:
      Revell, 1925.

1130 _____ . Seen in a Mexican Plaza: A Summer's
      Idyll of an Idle Summer. New York: Revell, 1918.
          Account of a visit to an isolated village.

1131 Wells, Carveth. Panamexico. New York: R.M. Mc-
      Bride, 1937.
          Account of a three-month trip from Panama
          through Mexico.

1132 Wells, David Ames. A Study of Mexico. New York:
      D. Appleton, 1887.

1133 Weston, Edward. The Daybooks... Vol. 1: Mexi-
      co, ed. Nancy Newhall. Rochester: George East-
      man House, 1961.
          Notes made by the American photographer during
          his years in Mexico City in the 1920's.

1134 Wheat, Marvin (pseud. Cincinnatus). Travels on the
      Western Slope of the Mexican Cordillera; In the
      Form of Fifty-One Letters, Descriptive of Much of
      This Portion of the Republic of Mexico.... San
      Francisco: Whitton, Towne, 1857.

1135 Whishaw, Lorna. Mexico Unknown. London: Ham-
      mond, Hammond, 1962.

1136 White, Philo. Narrative of a Cruize in the Pacific to
     South America and California on the U.S. Sloop-of-
     War Dale, 1841-1843, ed. Charles Lewis Camp.
     Denver: Old West, 1965.

1137 Whitworth, William B. Under an Aztec Sun: Adven-
     tures in Mexico. New York: Vantage, 1965.

1138 Wibberley, Leonard Patrick O'Connor. Yesterday's
     Land: A Baja California Adventure. New York:
     Washburn, 1961.
     Account of a trip made by the Irish-American.
     See also 525-526.

1139 Wilkes, Charles. Narrative of the United States Ex-
     ploring Expedition during the Years 1838, 1839,
     1840, 1841, 1842. Philadelphia: C. Sherman, 1844.

1140 Wilkins, James Hepburn. A Glimpse of Old Mexico;
     Being the Observations and Reflections of a Tender-
     foot Editor While on a Journey in the Land of Monte-
     zuma. San Rafael, Calif.: 1901.

1141 Willard, Theodore Arthur. The City of the Sacred
     Well; Being a Narrative of the Discoveries and Ex-
     cavations of Edward Herbert Thompson in the Ancient
     City of Chi-Chen Itza, with Some Civilization as Re-
     vealed by Their Art and Architecture.... London:
     W. Heinemann, 1926; New York, London: Century,
     1926.
     See also 528-529.

1142 Wilson, Henry Lane. Diplomatic Episodes in Mexico,
     Belgium, and Chile. Garden City: Doubleday, Page,
     1927; London: W. Heinemann, 1927.
     Memoir by the American ambassador 1909-1913.

1143 Wilson, James A. Bits of Old Mexico. San Francisco:
     1910.

1144 Wilson, Robert Anderson. Mexico and Its Religion,
     with Incidents of Travel in That Country during
     Parts of the Years 1851-52-53-54.... New York:
     Harper, 1855.

1145 Winter, Nevin Otto. Mexico and Her People To-Day:
     An Account of the Customs, Characteristics, Amuse-
     ments, History, and Advancement of the Mexicans,

and the Development and Resources of Their Country.
Boston: L.C. Page, 1907; London: Cassell, 1913.
Interpretation of present situation.

1146 Wise, Henry Augustus. Los Gringos, or An Inside
View of Mexico and California, with Wanderings
in Peru, Chili, and Polynesia. London: 1849;
New York: Baker & Scribner, 1849.

1147 Wislizenus, (Frederick or Friedrich) Adolphus. Memoir of a Tour to Northern Mexico Connected with
Col. Doniphan's Expedition in 1846 and 1847. Washington: Tippin & Streeper, 1848.

1148 Wolcott, Roger, ed. The Correspondence of William
Hickling Prescott, 1833-1847. Boston: Houghton
Mifflin, 1925.
Contains letters from Frances Calderón de la
Barca and others in Mexico.

1149 Wonderful Adventures: A Series of Narratives of
Personal Experiences among the Native Tribes of
America. London: Cassell, Petter & Galpin, 1872;
Philadelphia: W.B. Evans, 1874 (?).
"A Zigzag Journey through Mexico," by (Thomas)
Mayne Reid. See also 392-397.

1150 Woodcock, George. To the City of the Dead: An Account of Travels in Mexico. London: Faber &
Faber, 1957.
Account of a journey made by the Canadian to
central Mexico and Oaxaca (Mitla).

1151 Wortman, Mary E. Vail, and Orville Wortman.
Bouncing Down to Baja. Los Angeles: Westernlore,
1954.

1152 Wright, Marie Robinson. Picturesque Mexico. Philadelphia: J.B. Lippincott, 1897.

1153 Wright, Norman Pelham. Mexican Kaleidoscope. London, Toronto: Heinemann, 1947.

1154 Wright, Thomas E. Into the Maya World. London:
Hale, 1969.

1155 Wynkoop, J.M., ed. Anecdotes and Incidents; Comprising Daring Exploits, Personal and Amusing

Adventures of the Officers and Privates of the Army, and Thrilling Incidents of the Mexican War.   Pittsburgh: 1848.

1156   Zinsser, Hans. As I Remember Him: The Biography of R.S.   Boston: Little, Brown, 1940; London: Macmillan, 1940.
      Fictionalized memoirs of the bacteriologist's work, including his visit to Mexico City in 1931, when he met Hart Crane.

135

138

140